Tori Richard

The First Fifty Years

TORI

Tori Richard
The First Fifty Years

By Jocelyn Fujii

RICHARD

TR Press
Honolulu, Hawaii

TORI RICHARD
THE FIRST FIFTY YEARS

By Jocelyn Fujii
Design by Bud Linschoten

Copyright © 2006 TR PRESS

Photo credits can be found on page 115.

All rights reserved. No part of this book
may be reproduced in any form or by any
electronic or mechanical means without
written permission from the publisher.

Josh Feldman, *instigator*
Donna Burns, *project coordinator*

Published by
TR PRESS
1334 Moonui Street
Honolulu, Hawai'i 96817

Produced by
HULA MOON PRESS, LLC
P.O. Box 11173
Honolulu, Hawai'i 96828-0039

Library of Congress Control
Number: 2006903598
ISBN 0-9785466-0-1

Printed by Everbest Printing Co., Ltd.,
China

Contents

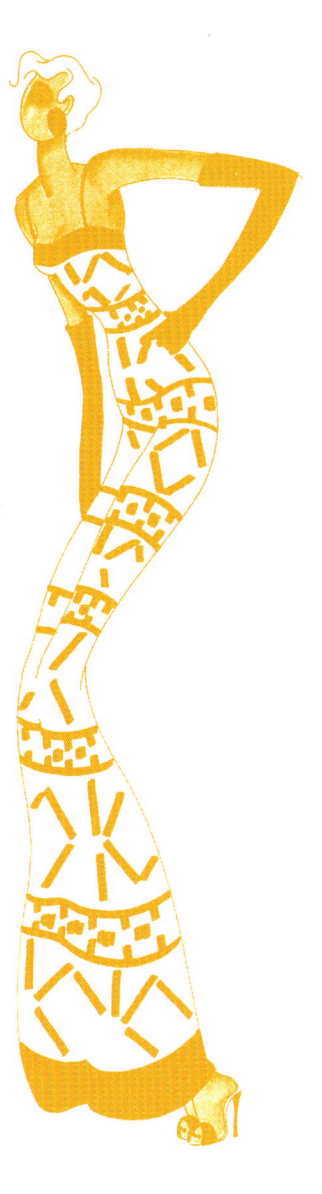

10   Curtains Up

16   The Endless Summer

34   The Art of the Print

48   Top Drawer

58   Tori Glory

66   Torigami

74   Grand Entrance

84   Play

92   Man of the House

106 Encore

114 Acknowledgments

115 References

115 Notes

115 Index

In the 1950s, Hawai'i was the darling of the nation. The legendary radio show "Hawai'i Calls" had been broadcasting from Waikīkī Beach since 1935, creating romance and longing for a U.S. territory on the cusp of statehood. Hollywood was churning out kitsch films like *Pagan Love Song* and somber classics like Oscar winner *From Here to Eternity*, and people like Frank Sinatra and Ava Gardner came to Waikīkī Beach for their honeymoons.

Curtains Up

Tori Richard's bold statements in print include Skoshi, an engineered print in polyester knit from 1969. Preceding page: an I. Magnin ad for Tori Richard from 1971.

Waikīkī beachboys ruled, even in Hollywood, where tanned surf gods like Harry Robello were members of the Screen Actors Guild and Olympic champion Duke Kahanamoku was as familiar an icon as Diamond Head.[1] Flocking to Hawai'i in swelling numbers, tourists were besotted with island fever, happily spreading their enthusiasm as they returned to their mainland homes.

Moving against the tide in this colorful milieu was an apparel manufacturer from Chicago, Mortimer Feldman. Unlike the tourists who came to Hawai'i, learned to surf, and returned in garish Hawaiian attire to their 1950s mainland lives, Feldman arrived in Hawai'i and never left. He flew to the Territory of Hawai'i on Pan American's China Clipper in 1953. He thought he would retire. Instead, three years later, he launched what became the hallmark of his life and a lasting signature, a resort apparel firm named Tori Richard.

With founding partners Janice Moody Robinson, who became his second wife, and pattern maker Mitsue Aka, Feldman defied convention by offering sophisticated women's fashions and strong, artistic prints over the typical, tropical "aloha wear" popular at the time. Tori Richard made national headlines and appeared in the finest retail stores in the country, from Fifth Avenue to San Francisco and beyond. Saks Fifth Avenue. Lord & Taylor. Bergdorf Goodman. I. Magnin. Neiman Marcus. Best & Co. Nordstrom. Marshall Field. Setting new standards for the industry from its Honolulu headquarters, Tori Richard established a reputation for excellence in fabrication, construction, and, most prominently, print as an art form.

While known for his aesthetic sensibilities, Mort Feldman also was uncannily savvy, prescient in his business decisions. When he returned to Tori Richard in 1994 after a 15-year "retirement," he brought with him his son, Josh Feldman, who would soon assume

Tori Richard founder Mort Feldman in the 1960s, below; and cotton sateen Tori Richard swimsuit and sundress, circa 1968, photographed at Mort Feldman's Honolulu home.

full responsibility for the company. Abandoning his plans for law school, the younger Feldman faced a nightmare scenario: demoralized employees, severely declining sales, grossly obsolete products, skyrocketing costs, and a deep state recession. The brand had been severely tarnished by fifteen years of neglect and absentee ownership. That decay had come to define the company and its products; the Tori Richard, Ltd. of 1994 was a shell of its former self. But with the father-and-son team, the turnaround was dramatic.

"Josh is proving himself invaluable to the company," reported *Island Business* magazine in 1998. "With his help, last year Tori Richard posted a 25 percent increase in Mainland and international sales."[2]

Most telling is the assessment of the founder himself, a man not given to praise. "We're probably still in business today because of Josh," he told Alison Frank of *Island Business*. "He's taken us in a new direction with his innovative thoughts, which are way beyond me, frankly."

Nearly 50 years after he established the company, Mort watched his "retirement" ease into its second generation with the same panache and fluidity that marked his arrival in 1953. When he died in November 2004, he was widely known as an icon in the local fashion world. "Entrepreneur had talent and heart," read the headline for his obituary in the *Honolulu Star-Bulletin*. "Mort Feldman…was considered by contemporaries as one of the most talented print designers that Hawaii has ever had in the apparel industry."

"He was a pioneer, a genius," said Jim Romig, chairman and founder of Hilo Hattie. "He was probably the most extraordinary textile designer that Hawai'i has ever had." While known for his impeccable taste and leadership in fashion—and his notorious volatility—Feldman was also a quiet philanthropist who gave generously and anonymously to nearly every solicitation that came his way.

Adapting to the times, proving that old school is the new school, the Feldman family business today enjoys unprecedented success and expansion as one of the oldest apparel manufacturers in Hawai'i. Women and men weaned on Tori Richard now see their grandchildren and great-grandchildren in its ever-evolving panoply of leisure wear, sold in thousands of stores across the country and in the premier resort destinations of Europe and Asia. Four Tori Richard retail stores have opened recently throughout Hawai'i. Under the younger Feldman's leadership, the company has achieved more than a 600 percent growth rate over the past several years.

But these are statistics, and for most of us, the joy of Tori Richard is in the seeing and the wearing. Like countless others, my own experience of Tori Richard is personal and nostalgic, rooted in the earliest moments of my fashion awareness as a child growing up on Kaua'i. My parents each had a closet full of Tori Richard designs: dramatic culottes, sharkskin Capri pants, jacquard pant sets, and Asian-inspired dresses for my mother; and shirts of memorable prints—koi and the Hokusai wave come to mind—that shared my father's closet space with Alfred Shaheen shirts. My parents prized these lines and wore them often. When the Coco Palms hotel was in its heyday, Sunday dinner there was a family ritual, and to my parents, Sunday best meant Tori Richard.

Today you can still see vintage Tori Richard turning up at concerts, on TV talk shows, on Kramer in an occasional *Seinfeld* re-run, and at graduations, weddings, and diverse social gatherings, worn by everyone from elderly "original owners" to young hipsters and urban professionals seasoned in the second-hand market. Your server at the trendy bistro, the one with the Prada sneakers and minimalist Oliver Peoples eyeglasses, might be wearing vintage Tori Richard, and so could your favorite local advertising executive. You can see contemporary Tori Richard fashions in the exotic resorts of the world, on entertainers, travelers and business

Tori Richard CEO Josh Feldman greets kupuna Nettie Tiffany, who conducted the blessing of Tori Richard's Ala Moana store in November, 2004.

Josh Feldman
Mort Feldman's son and president and CEO of Tori Richard

"Nearly all of my father's skills were self-taught and fought for. His success in life was possible only in this country. He tried to teach me as much as my stubborn youth would allow. He taught me how to appreciate the beautiful and the lovely, things like good design, art, architecture, ice cream, winning. Growing up and working with him was also a constant lesson in humility and humor.

"While he achieved material success, he never took it for granted, and he tried to make sure that his children didn't either. He was fervent in his belief in charity. He had a series of shoeboxes near his desk, each one filled to the brim with solicitations from untold organizations. All would get their due, usually anonymously. He felt that charity was an obligation of everyone, not a choice. And that it was best done anonymously."

people who appreciate the company's trademark prints and peerless quality in all phases of construction.

Integral to every part of Tori Richard are the skills and commitment of its employees, many of whom have worked there for two, three and nearly four decades. Not many companies can lay claim to that kind of loyalty and longevity. From art to design to sales, production, packing, and shipping, each employee's eye and hand have contributed to the finished product. Mort Feldman treated his employees as family and cared for them as passionately as he collected art.

That a Hawai'i business could thrive locally, maintain its national profile, and remain fresh and contemporary through half a century is reason enough to celebrate. But more than a book of fashion, the Tori Richard story is an intimate look at a company that helped to define a style and category of dress. It's the story of how a father and son, working together, averted their company's almost certain demise and brought it back from the brink.

Jocelyn Fujii

As reflected in the dramatic prints, modified kimono sleeves, and built-in belts of these 1973 dresses, Tori Richard built its reputation on print quality and East-West elements.

He had the eye of a perfectionist and a passion for art. From across a crowded antiques shop, he could spot an aesthetic detail and envision it on the flat surface of a textile, and then on the human body. It could have been a brush stroke on a Japanese screen or the corner of a Turkish carpet. It could have been the crest on a kimono or the particular glaze of a ceramic vase. For Mortimer Feldman, art was life and life was art, and there was little that could not be translated into the world of apparel he created as Tori Richard.

The Endless Summer

Vogue magazine in 1970 featured this Tori Richard outfit.

The Endless Summer

'Mort Feldman looked at wearable art back in the '50s and '60s, long before most people thought about it," says Lauren Yep, a merchandise team manager for Macy's and former Island Men's buyer for both Liberty House and Macy's. "That's what made him an innovator in the industry. He spared no expense when it came to investing in art and designing merchandising."

At its fifty-year mark, continues Yep, who has worked with Tori Richard for 18 years, "It's still one of the largest manufacturers that I do business with. Tori Richard is really a line that is internationally known."

With his inherent good taste, sense of adventure, and sound business instincts, Mort Feldman parlayed his humble beginnings into a storybook of upward mobility. When he died on November 8, 2004 at 83 years old, he left a rich legacy: He had established a thriving company, designed and built a sailboat, sailed to far horizons, and amassed an extensive collection of Japanese antiques and screens. He had broken a cartel. He had "retired" twice and teetered at the brink of bankruptcy. He had inspired loyalty and admiration—and a fair share of fear—among all those who knew him.

Bottom: *A modified Quonset hut was one of TR's earliest offices fifty years ago. Mitsue Aka, middle, and Mort and Janice Feldman, top, were the three founding partners of the company.*

A self-made man, he could not have predicted the success and longevity of his future company when he arrived in Hawai'i in 1953. A native of Boston, Massachusetts, he had had a hardscrabble youth about which only snippets are known: that he was a virtual orphan, moving from relative to relative until he left Boston at 15; that he enlisted in the Army Air Corps during World War II; and that, after the military, he sold apparel in the Midwest as a traveling salesman and displayed a natural creativity and an innate sense of style.

"After the war there were tremendous shortages, and he used to tell me how he'd go by streetcar to stores throughout Chicago and get orders," recalled his son, Josh Feldman, CEO of Tori Richard. "On his first day on the job, he got so many orders he was ecstatic. He had never seen anything like it: all these orders from all these stores for all these garments. He was going to buy a house; it was like winning a lottery.

"And then, a day later, his company said they couldn't produce any of it because there was a shortage of raw materials." He did manage to be successful once the scarcity problems were solved. Eventually he bought a factory that made children's outerwear, including coats made of surplus St. Mary's blankets. By the time he came to Hawai'i to visit a friend in windward O'ahu, at age 32, he was a successful and seasoned businessman.

Or was he? He was always, the younger Feldman notes, "a big enigma," and if his previous success was questionable, it soon became moot and irrelevant.

Upon arriving in Hawai'i and driving over the Old Pali Road with his friend, Feldman fell under the spell of the Ko'olau Mountains. Finding their dramatic escarpments evocative of the Tarzan movies he loved, he decided to retire in Hawai'i. His eye for quality proved dead-on once again. The beauty of Hawai'i captured his heart: summers became endless and winters a thing of the past. When they reached Lanikai, a catamaran waited on the beach. There were Mai Tais, and sailing, and soon a phone call to his first wife, Barbara Opperman, in Chicago. She agreed to join him in a new life in the Territory of Hawai'i.

Three years later, in 1956, Feldman established Tori Richard with Janice Moody Robinson, who became his second wife. A former clothing designer for Catalina Sportswear in California, she had been in the first graduating class in fashion design at the University of

Below right: *Mort and Janice Feldman on a photo shoot at the edge of the Waiʻalae Golf Course.*

Below middle: *National Neiman Marcus and Nordstrom ads feature Tori Richard fashions in 1972.*

California at Los Angeles in 1949. The third partner in Tori Richard was Mitsue Aka, who had been working with Moody as patternmaker. Each brought formidable talents to the new company.

From the beginning, the company was unconventional. It started with one sewing machine, three employees, and practically zero capital. Through the years its offices included a room on the pier at Honolulu Harbor, a Quonset hut, and a historic brewery. The first office, fondly remembered for the way the high tide dampened its floorboards, was at Pier 7 near the Aloha Tower in downtown Honolulu. The Quonset hut was next, on Beretania Street near the Honolulu Academy of Arts, and the brewery came in the late 1960s, after a long, more conventional stint on Keʻeaumoku Street.

Even the company's name was idiosyncratic. Who was Tori Richard anyway, this flamboyant upstart suddenly making waves across the country? Few people knew that Tori Richard was not one person, but two. Named after Victoria, Moody's daughter, who was nicknamed Tori, and Richard, Feldman's oldest son, Tori Richard was a name with legs. It had an aura, it struck a chord. It matched its target market and helped cement the company's identity.

"I was very young at the time they formed the company," recalls Tori Wickland, who was five years old when Feldman became her stepfather. "I remember being in a playpen in a big cutting room where they made patterns. One of the special clients that Tori Richard had was Lucille Ball. According to the stories, she had a very difficult figure to fit because her shoulders were wide. She had her resort outfits designed by my mom when

Karen MacRae
private label project coordinator

"Mort Feldman had such a sense. There was a stack of what we call strike-offs, the test printing on fabric, sitting on someone's desk. There was one that was particularly bad. The colors were awful. This other woman and I stuck it in the middle of the pile, scrunched up so you couldn't really see it. We didn't want to show it to him. He came into the office, glanced at the stack, and immediately picked it out. Immediately. It was scary.

"His famous line was, 'I wouldn't wear this to a dog show.'"

Cotton piqué dresses from 1970, photographed at Mort Feldman's Makiki Heights home.

Tori Richard swimsuits and beach wear, photographed in 1964, four years before the company discontinued swimwear.

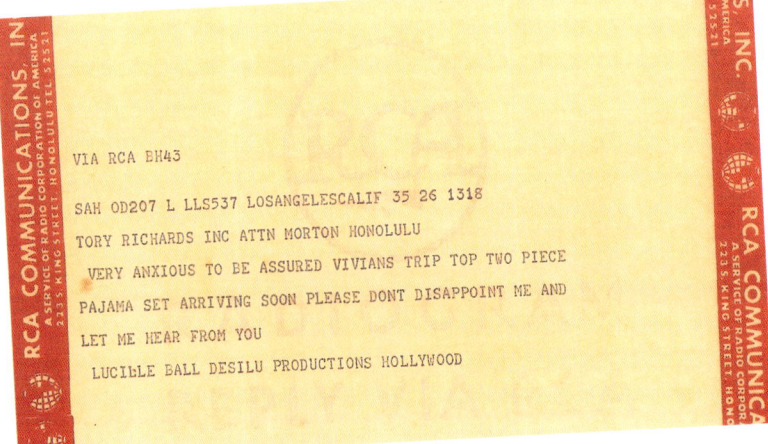

Lucille Ball, with her slim waist and broad shoulders, was one of Tori Richard's prominent clients.

she was in the Islands. She would be fitted at the Royal Hawaiian, where they stayed. My mother cut and designed a lot of things uniquely for her and the time."

Hawai'i was looking west at the time—it was three years before statehood—and from its inception, Tori Richard staked its claim as a company that was based in Hawai'i but not limited to it. It was not, as Josh Feldman would stress decades later, "defined by products that were hula-girl or palm-tree driven.

"Although many people today associate us with men's wear, we began with women's fashions that were nationally known," notes Feldman. "We have always been a resort wear company that made dramatic prints."

"We were located in Hawai'i, but we were not doing aloha prints," adds Bobbie Taum, who worked at Tori Richard for a total of 18 years, most of them as Feldman's administrative assistant. "The Tori Richard concept was a garment that could take you anywhere, anytime."

Tori Richard's offices in key mainland markets—New York, California, Dallas, Chicago, Florida—brought national headlines, advertisements and window displays. By the early 1960s, the Tori Richard summer line was on display at places like the Savoy Hilton at

Gimbel's department store windows in New York featured Tori Richard women's wear in 1961, while Saks Fifth Avenue, in 1968, and I. Magnin, in 1971, ran stylish Tori Richard loungewear ads.

Fifth Avenue and 58th St. in New York. I. Magnin, Lord & Taylor, Neiman Marcus and other top-notch retailers were quick to glom the line.

The company's resort high fashion titillated fashion editors with its bold prints, innovative colors, and classic, uncluttered silhouettes. It was a time when clothes were "fetching," "winsome," "gay," "chic" and "sunlovable." In 1970, *Vogue* ran an eight-page marketing spread on Tori Richard, photographed in Hawai'i, featuring Penelope Tree and other top models of the time. In lavish photo spreads shot on location, made-in-Hawai'i fashions were featured in *Harper's Bazaar*, *Mademoiselle*, *Glamour*, *Life*, *Town & Country*, and other significant publications of the day.

While playful, Tori Richard garments were seriously fashionable, sparing no expense in textile art, fabric, and workmanship. Large, bold textile designs were engineered to fit each garment, matching fronts and pockets so that the prints remained uninterrupted in the final piece. These "engineered prints" were technically complex and visually dramatic, often featuring an image that was printed 60 inches wide. Tori Richard's high-end dresses, shifts, and sports and beach wear sprang to life in fabrics like

Previous page: Tori Richard's white cotton embossed jacquard dress from the mid-1960s is photographed on the grounds of 'Iolani Palace. Below, Mort and Janice Feldman review designs with a Saks Fifth Avenue buyer, 1961. Right and below: a peekaboo sundress and silk dupioni harem skirt are Tori Richard's take on play.

"Trentine," a French cotton that combined two prints in each garment: shaded green stripes on the border and white dots on bright pink. Yardage from Paris, West Germany and the Netherlands was imported for Tori Richard styles that sold briskly nationwide. Cottons and silks in various weights and textures bore classic motifs such as bold stripes and floral, border and tropical prints on the best fabrics of the day. In their dramatic, often Asian-inspired fabric prints and silhouettes, the cotton sateen, piqué, dobbies (fabrics with small geometric figures woven into them) and silks made powerful aesthetic statements.

Throughout America, the beach, patio and cocktail party were the epicenters of leisure, and Tori Richard was happy to oblige. "Hostess wear" and the A-line silhouette were the rage. Drawing inspiration from around the world, particularly Europe and Asia, the Tori Richard style stood out. Capri pants, Mandarin collars, black-and-white hostess sets, culottes, caftan-type shifts, sarong swimsuits, kabuki-sleeved tunics, harem pants, and, yes, the muʻumuʻu with an edge, got people's attention in Hawaiʻi and abroad.

"It was a dynamic combination,"

Vintage dresses from the 1960s feature dynamic motifs, below. Lower right: an I. Magnin ad in 1971, and following page, Tori Richard in a Frost Brothers ad from 1970.

recalls Leonard Poliandro, a crackerjack salesman and textile expert, now retired in Massachusetts, who worked for Tori Richard in the 1960s and '70s. "Janice with her styling, Mitsue with her patternmaking, and Mort. He was great at doing business and watching the costs, and he had good taste.

"My area was sales, finding what the market wanted. At that time Tori Richard was all women's wear. They wanted large prints, but they didn't want Hawaiian dumb prints. Some garment manufacturers were coming out with silly prints. My feedback was that the market wanted sophistication."

Poliandro accompanied the Feldmans to Europe, returned to New York, and sold the line based on the artwork—before it was even printed. "It was a tremendous advantage," said Poliandro. He succeeded in securing orders from Saks, Lord & Taylor, Bergdorf, and other Fifth Avenue stores.

With Island manufacturers Alfred Shaheen, Iolani, Kamehameha, Malia and Kahala, Tori Richard also figured prominently in the local economy. According to Linda B. Arthur in her book *Aloha Attire*, "The late 1950s through the 1960s was a period of unprecedented growth for the Hawaiian fashion industry."[1]

The industry was born "in backyard garages and home sewing rooms and has grown faster than any of Hawai'i's economic children since World War II," wrote *The Beacon* in April 1962. Under the headline "Hawaii's Glamour Garments," the article outlined the burgeoning importance of the industry: $918,000 worth of garment sales in 1950 and $19,600,000 in 1960, an annual growth of 36 percent.[2] By comparison, tourism showed only an 18.4 percent annual advance in that period. "Fashion is big business in America today," the article went on. "Last year more than $40 *billion* was spent for clothes." In 1962, the apparel industry was Hawai'i's third largest export.

"Quality is the reason mainland stores will buy things, other than *muumuus*, from a manufacturing source separated by 2,000 miles of ocean," Mort Feldman, then the Hawaiian Fashion Guild's vice president, told *The Beacon*. "As one of a dozen or so firms that have hurdled the aloha shirt/*muumuu* barrier, Tori Richard's Mort Feldman sells Saks Fifth in New York better dresses…" *The Beacon* continued, naming as other pioneers Kahala, then owned by Nat Norfleet Sr., and Malia Hawaii, owned by Bill and Mary Foster.

Statehood in 1959 opened the

Tori Richard goes to the beach at the Royal Hawaiian Hotel, below; to the harbor, below right; and to the heights of fashion in ads by Saks Fifth Avenue in 1964, Jordan Marsh in 1965, and Bergdorf Goodman in 1971.

door to jet travel, accelerated resort development, and heightened tourism, which was on its way to becoming the number-one industry in the state in 1976.[3] By the early 1960s, Tori Richard was sold in France, Britain, Belgium, Germany, Australia, Hong Kong, India—all over the world. Elected vice president of the Hawaiian Fashion Guild in 1962 and president two years later, Feldman stepped up his advocacy for the industry as well as for his burgeoning company.

In the mid-1960s, Tori Richard's 200 mainland outlets constituted 75 percent of its business. Despite the rise of his own company, Feldman had fears that Hawai'i's apparel industry might be in a downturn as the honeymoon of statehood receded. In 1964, Feldman told *The Honolulu Advertiser* that the industry, at about $25 million, may have declined about 15 percent from the peak reached about 18 months after statehood. The setback, however, proved to be temporary. In 1977, according to *California Apparel News*, the industry was showing "continual growth over the years, from $33.7 million in sales to $60 million."[4]

In 1962, when Howard Hope of Sun Fashions was president of the Hawaiian Fashion Guild and Mort Feldman was vice president, the

Hawai'i State Legislature formally urged the use of "Aloha" wear through the summer months. Five years later, the Legislature adopted a resolution officially adopting "Aloha Friday." The concept was a huge boost to the local garment industry, particularly the men's wear manufacturers, because it urged Islanders to wear aloha shirts every Friday year-round, even in the stuffy banks and boardrooms of downtown Honolulu's Bishop Street.

In adapting to the changes in the industry, Feldman achieved unqualified success in several ways. By bypassing five companies that had a lock on Japanese textile imports, he broke a cartel and established his own contacts with the oldest and finest mills in Japan. One of those mills developed a fabric with Feldman that came to be known as "polyester suede," a best-seller identified with the disco era, a time when the fabrics were as slick as the hair, and synthetics ruled the world.

Along with "Aloha Friday," the request of local retailer Liberty House made Tori Richard men's wear inevitable. By popular demand, using some of its leading women's prints for men's shirts, Tori Richard launched its men's wear line in 1969 and watched it gallop ahead of its women's line by the early 1980s.

"Polyester suede was the 100 percent 'bulletproof' shirt that everyone owned," comments Lauren Yep, industry veteran and former Liberty House buyer. "I think every businessman in town owned one. Even in the late '80s and '90s, we used to go through thousands of units of those shirts. You'd never think it would have that kind of longevity."

"Mort set a new standard with those polyester prints for men and women," adds Nat Norfleet Jr., whose father founded Kahala, one of Hawai'i's first garment manufacturers, and who worked at Tori Richard in 1976. "If you went to a cocktail party in Hawai'i in the '70s and '80s, the men almost always wore a Tori Richard shirt. His taste was in his choice of prints. He developed them exclusively in Japan, where they had the best printing techniques in the world. Mort's taste always surrounded him, dramatically."

Despite the success of their company, the Feldmans divorced, and Janice Feldman left the company in 1967, never to design again. She died ten years later. Haruko Moberg, a talented Japanese designer, had apprenticed under Janice Feldman and stayed with the company until 1972. With Mort Feldman's penchant for the art and

The old Primo Brewery on Cooke Street, the Tori Richard headquarters from 1968 to 1990, was damaged by fire in 1973.

Bobbie Taum
former assistant to Mort Feldman

"He was so colorful, so creative, and he gave everyone the opportunity to excel. He was open to ideas. He was very open with his criticisms. The important thing is, you knew exactly where you stood with him. If you couldn't take it, you didn't belong here.

"In order to survive, you had to have the willingness to see through all of this for the end product. It was all about learning to be involved in the creative process."

Cotton sateen was popular in Tori Richard swimwear throughout the 1960s

aesthetics of Japan, and with his network of Japanese contacts, Moberg helped to further infuse the line with strong Asian influences in her textile and clothing designs. "I think that every year I created about 100 new fabrics," Moberg recalls. "Each one was a minimum of 3,000 yards and some, up to 20,000 yards."

Dedicated showrooms in Atlanta, Chicago, Dallas, Los Angeles and New York kept the women's line highly visible and in the finest stores in the country. The company kept up its own level of in-house glamour. Tori Richard's new office, the old Primo Brewery on Cooke Street, added to the excitement. It wasn't just an office building; it was a historic brewery, 89 years old at the time, and it was a personal passion of Feldman's and one of his prominent real estate projects with business partner Bob Cosco. The 68,000-square-foot property cost a half-million dollars to renovate and was written up in business, real estate and feature articles. And it was Tori Richard's new home, a showcase for Feldman's growing collection of Japanese screens and Asian antiques.

On May 12, 1973, a fire struck the Cooke Street building. Originating at a furniture store on the first floor, it damaged Tori Richard's entire inventory of finished goods and

Vogue magazine's 1970 Hawai'i spread featured Tori Richard fashions at the beach, sailing, and at Maui's 'Iao Valley, bottom.

fabric, most of it smoke, water and soot damage. The loss to Tori Richard was over $500,000, but that did not stop the public from thronging the factory for reduced merchandise. A "fire sale" ensued, causing a stampede of customers that tied up traffic on the H-1 freeway. Long lines snaked around the block. "The lines were so long that back at the end, no one knew which line she was in," wrote Lois Taylor in *the Honolulu Star-Bulletin*. "Nobody gave up, though, for the simple reason that the bargains were real."[5] After costly renovations, the company remained at the site for 17 more years.

In the mid-1970s, Feldman hired June Tatibouet and gave her the title of "merchandise stylist." As with all others he believed in, he gave her the chance to prove herself—and she did. In charge of concept and direction for women's wear, she seized upon the loungewear trend and developed quilted robes for Tori Richard. More significantly, she introduced cotton lawn, a high-quality Egyptian cotton that remains one of Tori Richard's biggest sellers to this day.

On October 21, 1981, *Honolulu Star-Bulletin* columnist Dave Donnelly gushed over Tori Richard loungewear's royal feat: "The Tori Richard ad campaign on the

Mark Troedson
Tori Richard Pacific marketing director

"I've worked at Tori Richard for over 25 years. I had been working at Iolani Sportswear for four years, and when I came here in 1980, Mr. Feldman supported me by allowing management to merchandise a line for me, Cooke Street, so that I could get out there and sell it… Others in the company, in 1980, said that I shouldn't be doing reverse prints. At 8 o'clock one night, while we were working in the art room discussing this, Mort said, 'Take a $50,000 bill, spend the money, see what this kid can do.' I'll never forget it. I was 31 years old. He supported me as a salesman, gave me the opportunity to show him that I could sell."

Mainland features an exotic silk loungewear collection with Oriental flair described as 'fit for an empress,' and the king of Morocco seems to have taken it at face value," he wrote. "The ambassador of Morocco phoned from Washington the other day and ordered—get ready, now!—four dozen of each style in the line for the 'royal household.' Tori Richard exec Stan Morketter is still vibrating—the bill came to well over $10,000."

The polyester trend waned in the '80s, replaced by a plethora of cottons and silks that complemented the Tori Richard image. Men's sportswear, in cotton lawn and other fabrics, eclipsed women's wear in sales volume and turned Tori Richard into a predominantly men's wear line. But in the early 1980s, a designer and stylist named Amos Kotomori toured the mainland for Tori Richard and injected a new sense of drama with his award-winning knitted women's fashions. In a Hawaiian Fashion Guild ad in 1982, Tori Richard was dubbed the "Cadillac of the Fashion Industry in Hawaii."

At the sales end of the business, a young new salesman named Mark Troedson was eager to make a difference. Hired in 1980 to develop the Cooke Street line for Tori Richard, Troedson was given a break by a man who was willing to take risks. "Mort supported me as a salesman and gave me the opportunity to show him what I could do," said Troedson, today the company's Pacific marketing director. Cooke Street and its reverse-style pullovers ended up being one of the biggest-selling shirts for Liberty House.

But the restless Feldman "retired" again, this time to New Zealand to build a boat and follow his dreams with June, by then his wife, and her 8-year-old son, Josh. In search of a new art form, Feldman built the boat, the 105-foot *Shere Khan*, and continued his retirement in typically lavish form: across continents. From 1983 to 1994, from New Zealand to Europe to a new home in Southern California, Mort Feldman's absence from his company created a palpable leadership vacuum. Only when he returned in 1994, with son Josh as his successor, did the company reclaim its legacy.

Suddenly the young boy who used to run around the office, play with the computers, and respectfully call employees "Mr." and "Mrs." returned to the company a mature, Mort-mentored executive. He got to the business of retooling the business by boosting its mainland market share and re-asserting the aesthetic legacy that had slipped during his father's absence.

"In 1994, we were doing 95 percent of our business in Hawai'i and 5 percent elsewhere, mostly the mainland," explained Feldman. "And only ten to fifteen years earlier, it would have been the opposite." Today Tori Richard's business is 80 percent mainland driven. Bright and energetic, a graduate of Punahou School and the University of California at San Diego, Josh Feldman has a degree in art and a degree in political science—and what seems like a genetic disposition to the complex dynamics of a family business. He possesses a preternatural eye for quality and has inherited his father's ethics. His sense of purpose is as much personal as professional, and his achievements have not been modest. A year after he joined the company in 1994, he reintroduced the engineered print, a Tori Richard innovation and a company bestseller today. Revenues and markets have multiplied. In 2001, at an international men's apparel trade show in Las Vegas called Magic, Tori Richard won an award for having the best booth design of 3,500 exhibitions from companies all over the world.

The Mort Feldman credo—adapt to the times—has segued into the next generation. With the dramatic growth of recent years, there's a new spring in the Tori Richard step. If fifty is the new thirty and prints are the new black, the next half-century will be a wild ride.

Geometrics and stylized motifs are popular in Tori Richard designs.

Summer
The Art of the Print

Kim Scoggins, former vice president and chief operating officer of Tori Richard, likes to tell the story of how a top-level decision with Nichimen Co., Ltd., a Japanese multinational, was made with the toss of a coin. On one of their frequent trips to Osaka, Japan, he and Mort Feldman found themselves working past midnight negotiating the price for a large purchase of unprinted fabrics, called greige goods.

"We were dealing with giant multinational trading companies with oil, finance, and manufacturing interests," he recalled. "Those were the glory days of Japan, the 1970s. We were negotiating a price for 500,000 yards, so even a penny a yard made a fairly large difference." Crucial to the discussion was the yen conversion rate, and whether or not Tori Richard would fix the loan or let it float.

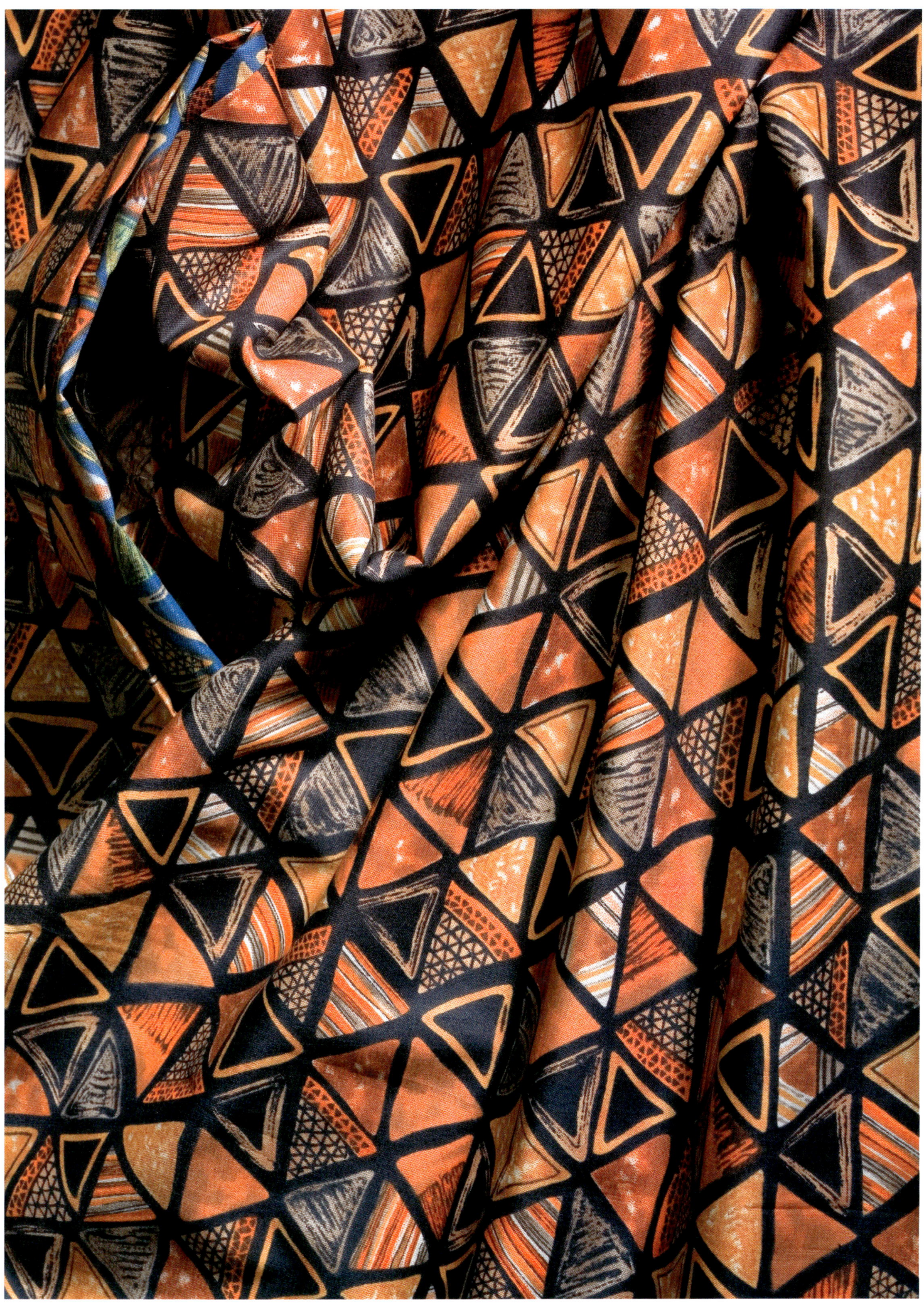

The Art of the Print

When both parties were close to agreeing, said Scoggins, "Mort looked at A. Kojoma, the Nichimen representative, and said, 'You're not going to change your price, and we're not necessarily happy with the price, so let's each pick a price that we're happy with. And we'll flip for it.'"

Kojoma-san's eyes lit up. He had been educated in America, and to him a coin toss was the quintessential American thing to do. A gamble. A flip of the coin. This was within his range of approval: Yes!

"He was so excited," continued Scoggins. "We flipped an American coin. Mort won. Kojoma turned pale white. The difference was about $15,000 in our favor. Then we went out for a snack."

Everyone who has traveled with Feldman has a story or two about his unorthodox modus operandi and his success in navigating the delicate, protocol-ridden labyrinth of the highly relationship-oriented business. "Mort had developed these relationships over a long time, and they saw him more as a relationship client than just a customer," said Scoggins. "Mort traveled to Japan for three weeks at a time, three or four times a year, for decades."

A Japanophile to the core, Mort

Preceding page: *Triad in cotton lawn, 2003*. This page: Mort and Janice Feldman in the early days of Tori Richard, above left, and *Daiquiri, a top-selling polyester suede print from 1970*, above.

Prints range from mini-geometrics in fine cotton lawn, right, to Tiare Tahiti in cotton broadcloth, far right. Orient Express, in silk and Tencel® in 2001, was a popular matched-front design, below.

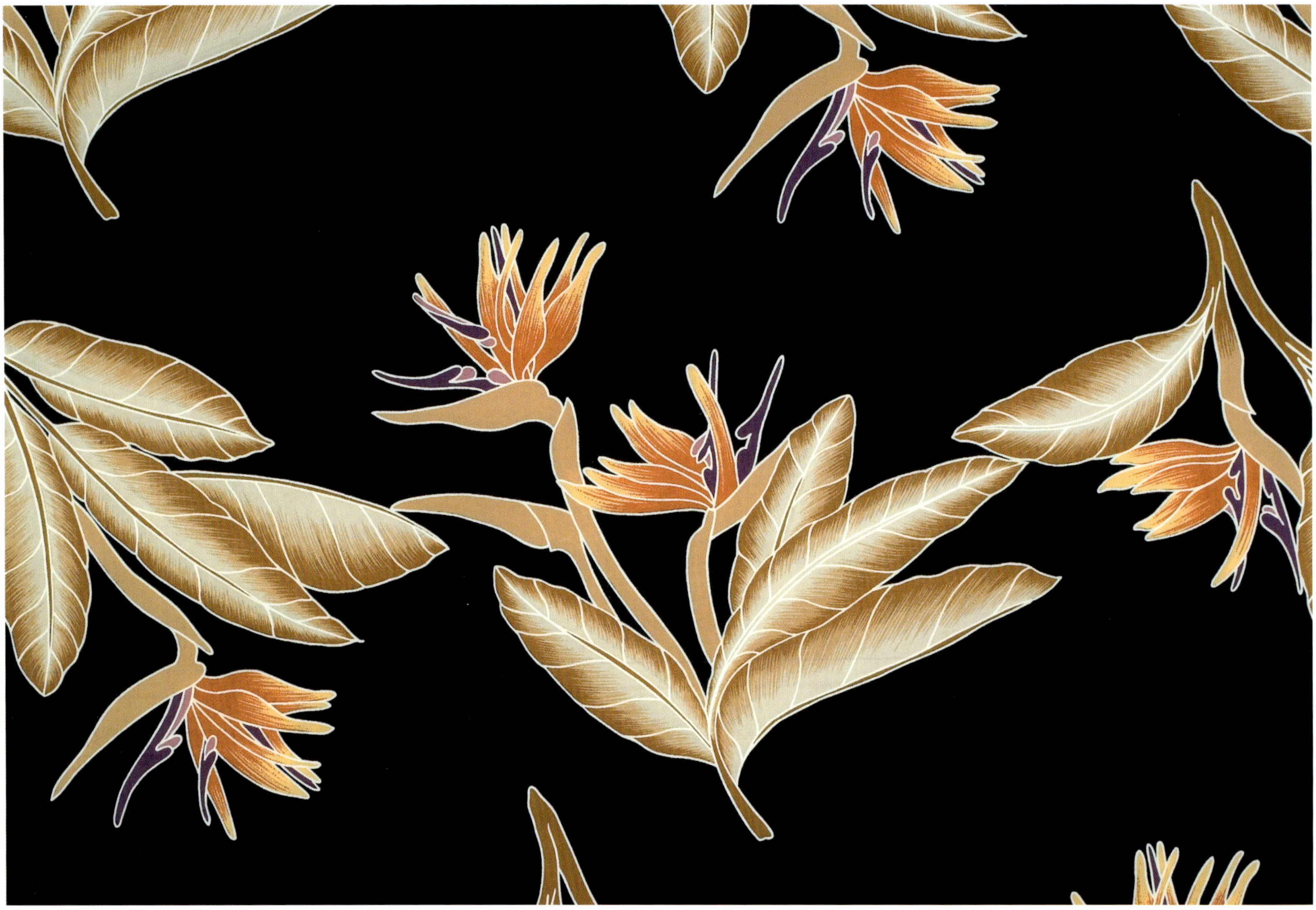

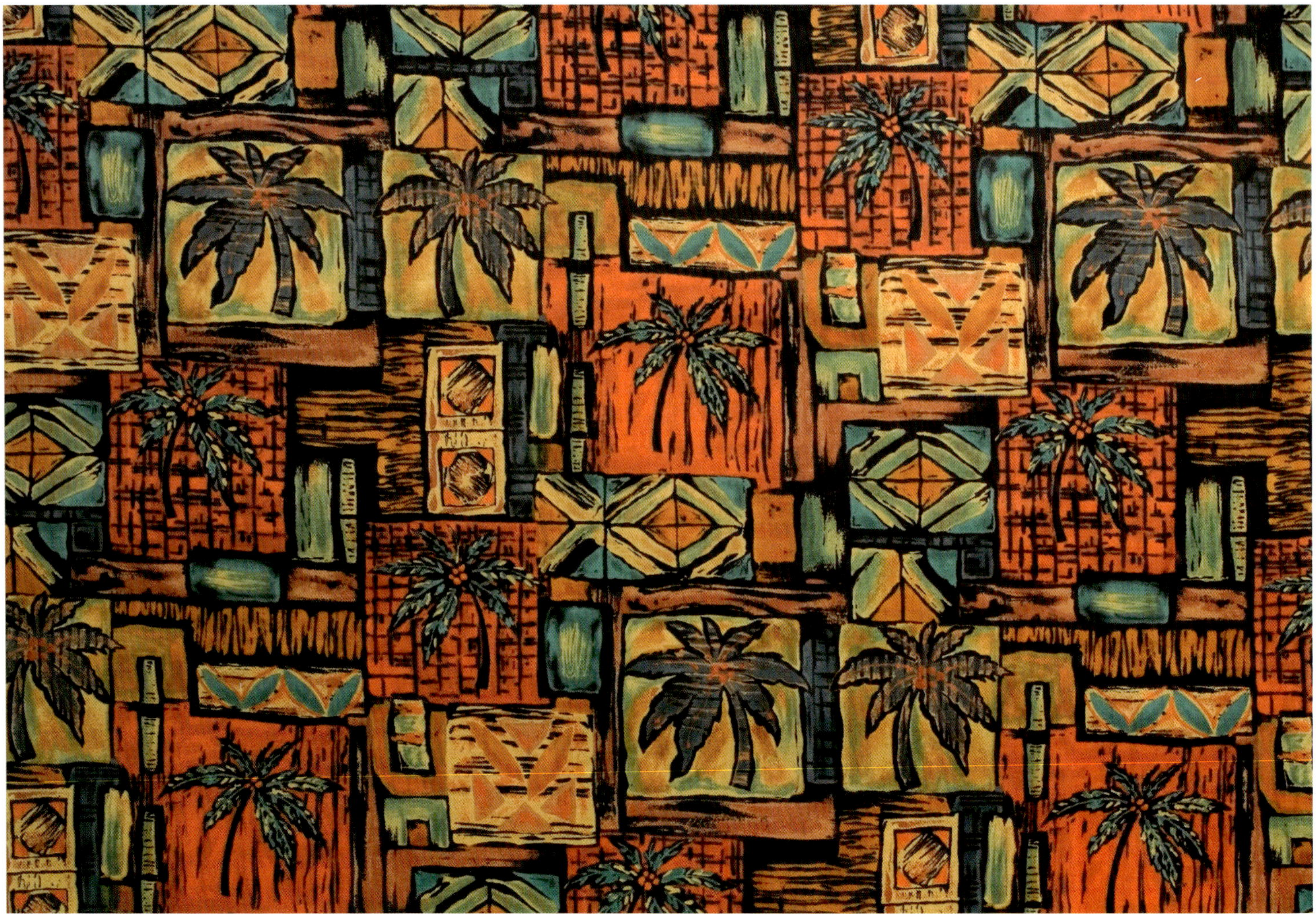

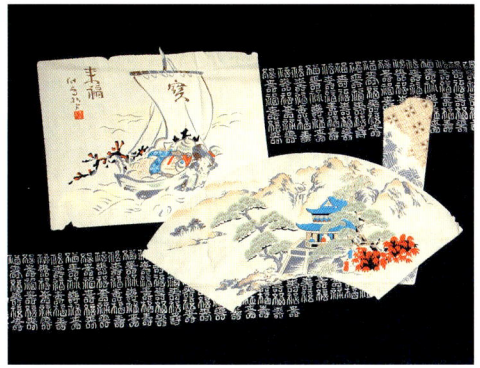

Feldman loved Japanese art, food, and aesthetics, passions that related naturally to his business. China had not yet entered the scene, and Japan made outstanding textiles, had sophisticated print technology, and possessed the aesthetics that were at one with his own. From the beginning, Feldman knew that Japan was essential to the quality and the volume that he sought for Tori Richard.

"In Hawai'i, all the manufacturers wanted their prints to be made in Japan," recalled Len Poliandro, who was vice-president of sales at Tori Richard in the 1960s. "At the time, if you did business nationally and were shipping coast-to-coast, you were considered topnotch. If you were doing business in Japan and shipping internationally, that was considered unbelievable.

"Normally the American printing minimums were 12,000 to 15,000 yards, and they only had enough screens for four to six colors. In Japan, you could print 3,000 yards and use eight, nine, twelve screens, up to eighteen—whatever you wanted. You could be more artistic with your prints, you could almost print a painting. These were the advantages that Mort picked up on because of his good taste and his understanding of

Preceding page: Maemae is a cotton poplin print from the early 1980s, top; Gauguin colors come in a 16-screen cotton lawn, bottom.

Clockwise from top left: a cotton broadcloth shirt print from the 1980s; a 1950s Asian motif, recently redone; and a 1970s polyester print, reintroduced on Tencel® in 1999. Right: Sushi in spun viscose, 1997.

Domino, right, was a popular cotton lawn print, and Cachet, middle and bottom, had cachet in the heyday of polyester suede.

all types of fabrics."

Moreover, added Poliandro, "Mort collected Japanese art and was very much in their mindset. Keeping his word was his bond; that was a very important thing. The Japanese are the same way. He was a tough negotiator, but once the agreement was set, he stayed by his word. It was easy for him to do because he was very, very honorable. And the Japanese are honorable."

In order to work with Japan, Feldman had to break with tradition. He became the first person in Hawai'i to bypass the middlemen and order textiles directly from the mills in Japan. Textiles were a huge industry in Japan after World War II, and Hawai'i was the gateway for its raw materials entering the continental U.S. At the time one of the U.S.'s largest textile suppliers, Japan opened official, government-approved mercantile offices in Hawai'i under the name Aloha Kai.[1]

"It was a cartel of five converters, or manufacturers, who went in right after the war and made a deal with the Japanese government to buy Japanese fabrics," explained Jim Romig, chairman and founder of Hilo Hattie. "No one could buy fabrics from Japan without going through them, or from someone else they sold to. We were determined to be able to buy our fabrics directly from Japan, and Mort pioneered it. It was a matter of economics and principle. He spent a lot of time and effort cracking the cartel."

Josh Feldman remembers his father telling him how he established this hard-won access. "My father described how he'd go to these mills in Japan and sit at the end of a long table with maybe thirty people," recalled the younger Feldman. "While negotiating with the guy next to him, he'd write something on a piece of paper and pass it to him. The guy next to him would write something else on the paper, and the note would go all the way down to the man at the end of

Japanese-inspired Kaze (wind), left, and Distant Island, below, reveal the possibilities of black in textile art.

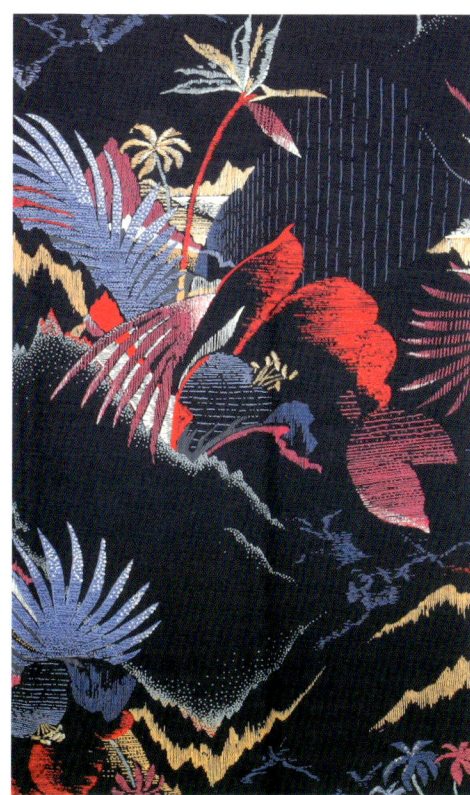

the table—who would be reading a newspaper and smoking a cigarette." Annoyed at the interruption, said Feldman, the decision-making honcho at the end of the table would write his note, which would then travel the long and cumbersome route back to the note's originator at the opposite end of the conference table.

"My dad would get very frustrated at these meetings. Finally, one of the guys took him aside and said, 'Feldman-san, I know what you want; meet me at this hotel.' He couldn't let anyone know he was going to break the cartel, that he was going to ship around it, but that's what happened."

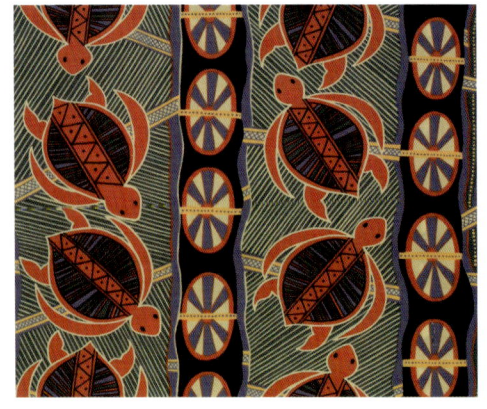

The skill of fabric coordinator Amy Renshaw is critical to the print design and selection process. Top, Wanderer reflects European influences, and Turtle, above, in cotton broadcloth, takes its cues from nature.

That breakthrough put Tori Richard on its way. Today the company is one of a handful of U.S. manufacturers who do their own converting, controlling all their means of production except for the actual printing process.

The nerve center of this enterprise is the Tori Richard headquarters on the outskirts of downtown Honolulu. On the second floor of the building, under twelve-foot-high ceilings, thousands of flat sheets of fabric hang in two tiers from individual metal dowels. The "keeps," as they're called, 45 or 60 inches long, dangle like flags stacked vertically in a section of the building called the archive. The keeps are a visual record, a complete collection of every Tori Richard print that has been created in the past half-century. Marquesas, Murano, Patio, Rio, Arabesque, Kenya, Seafrost, Tegaki, Shibui, Kabuki, Plaza, Sunrise, Pop!—they're all there, some 15,000 prints, growing by about 400 a year, each with its own name and provenance and its own place in Tori Richard history. If there is anything close to what could be called the DNA of the company, this is it.

As extensive as the archive is, said Feldman, it is a mere fraction of what comes through Tori Richard's doors. As a print-driven operation, Tori Richard applies exacting standards at every stage to what will ultimately appear as a finished product. By the time the art is created, the colors are chosen, the fabric is printed, and the garment is shaped and sewn, a host of aesthetic and technological factors have come into play. The art of the print, says Feldman, is the genesis of the line, the place where it all begins.

"We create prints according to certain criteria and rules," noted Feldman. "One of those criteria, aesthetic balance, requires that the motifs be in proportion, that nothing 'jumps' off the piece." Some of the rules he would not reveal. "Another is: How much work will be necessary to make the design

The ethnic imagery of Lima, left, in cotton lawn; Hulu, below, in viscose; and Pine Forest and Tsuru, middle and bottom, acknowledge cultures from around the world.

technically correct? A complicated print can involve up to 100 man hours just in making the art printable. Is the artwork relevant? What kind of fabrication will the print ultimately end up on? Most importantly, is the art special or redundant? If a similar look is in the marketplace or we have done something before, we generally avoid it."

Every print is copyrighted, given a name, and is the exclusive property of Tori Richard. Some fabrics are not only printed in Tori Richard designs, but are woven in special patterns and weaves that also have been designed by in-house artists. Some, such as the cotton lawn, are given an exclusive special finish, and these features, too, are proprietary and protected by long-term agreements with suppliers.

When trademark and copyright infringements are discovered, they are pursued, says Feldman. A vigilant protector of his company's creative product, Feldman has found bootlegged Tori Richard fabrics and prints for sale at trade shows, in retail outlets, and even on E-bay on the Internet. "It's pretty common for Josh to go to a mainland trade show and, all of a sudden, call me from the show and say, 'So-and-so has one of our shirt print designs and is taking orders off of it,'" recounted Martin Hsia, the company's patent attorney. "We have had situations in which the designs were not just a copy of our print, but of the actual shirt."

In the last decade, the company has successfully settled twenty infringement cases, among them a bathrobe in a Tori Richard print, sold by Phillips-Van Heusen. The case, settled by Knothe, Phillips-Van Heusen's licensee, is just one example of the slippery slope of copyright infringement.

It's no wonder the designs are so carefully guarded: The creative and technical process is at the core of the company's identity and is complex, time-consuming and demand-

*Details of foliage, below, and fire (*Waterway*, top) and water (*Wavelength*, bottom), following page, are captured in two dimensions with Tori Richard's print technology.*

ing. The first step in printing, the concept art, may be inspired by original work from European studios and far-flung destinations reflecting a sophisticated lifestyle and aesthetic. In a confluence of technology and artistic sensibility, printing translates these elements into textile and creates wearable art. This was Mort Feldman's forte. He made regular trips to Paris, France, and Como, Italy, where he perused thousands of pieces of original art as inspiration for a part of the print line. He traveled to Asia and walked down cobblestone alleys and hidden passageways to discover antiques and art treasures that would stoke the creative fires. Traveling in his father's footsteps, with his own sure instincts for art and lifestyle, Josh Feldman embraces and modernizes that legacy.

The actual print is created in-house, in a complex process that involves lively brainstorming among Tori Richard artists and designers. They carefully consider colors, design, fabrication, season, and "repeat," a term that refers to the placement of the design on the fabric and how often it will have to be repeated.

The number of color screens is integral to the sophistication and possibilities of each print. "We use up to seventeen screens on viscose. On silk, we can do up to twenty-two," explained Amy Renshaw, coordinator of the fabric department, who has worked at the company since 1979. "On cotton lawn, we typically use fifteen screens, and we add a special finish that belongs exclusively to Tori Richard."

The original concept design is printed in repeat in Japan, she continued. "Usually our repeat is 24 to 30 inches, and up to 60 inches for the large engineered prints. The repeat has to be seamless from top to bottom and from side to side. When they paint the full repeat of the design, what we call the master sketch, they also paint croquis, called colorways."

The staff reviews the croquis and adjusts the colors, a process that could result in two or three more cycles of corrections. After they're approved, they are sent back to the printer for a strike-off, a test print of the design on fabric.

It's a lengthy process, and when applied to every one of the hundreds of prints the company produces a year, a picture of intricacy and complexity appears. Each step of the print process is repeated hundreds of times a year.

Tori Richard seamstresses sew the samples, but the bulk of the apparel construction is contracted outside of the company. "The

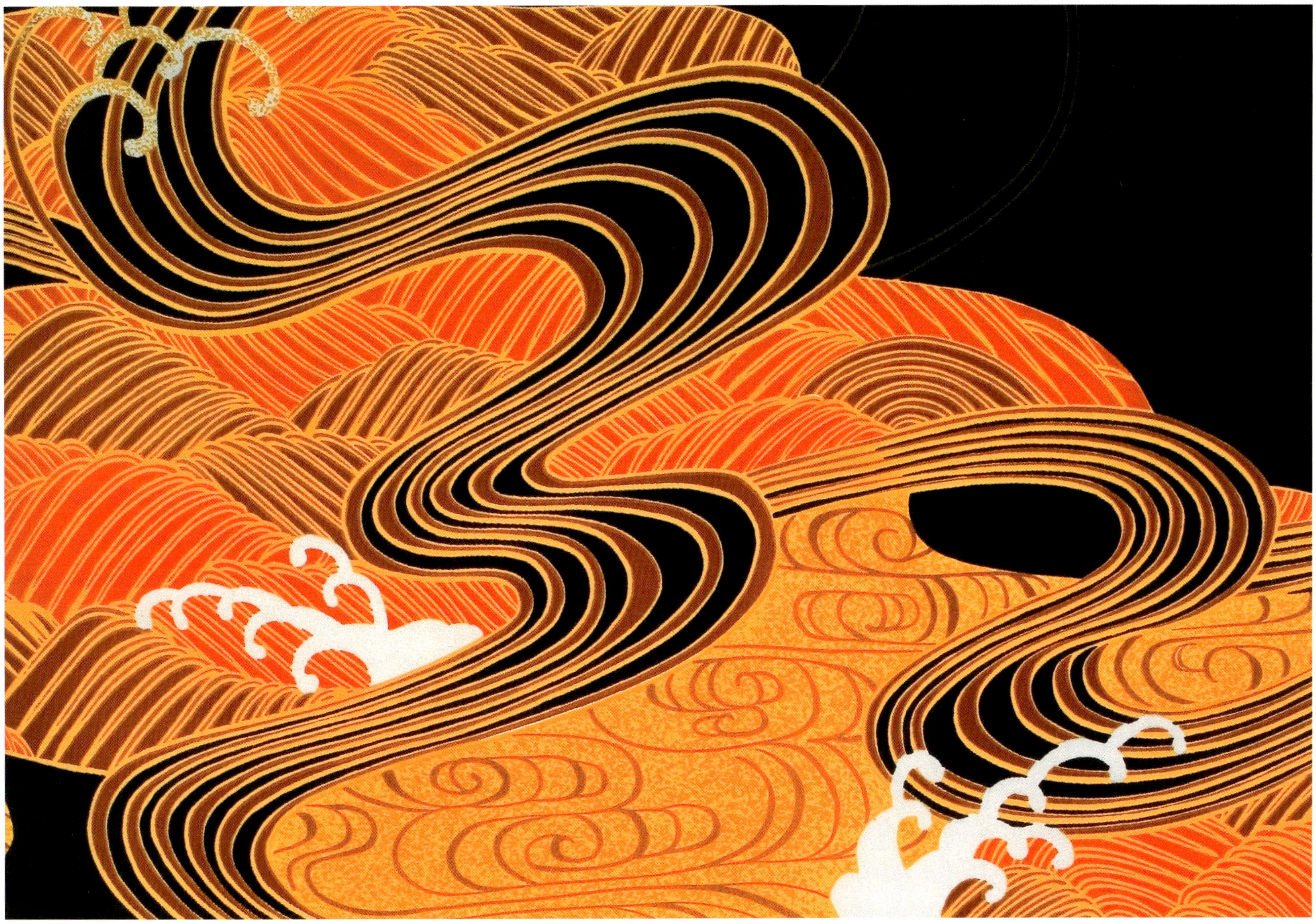

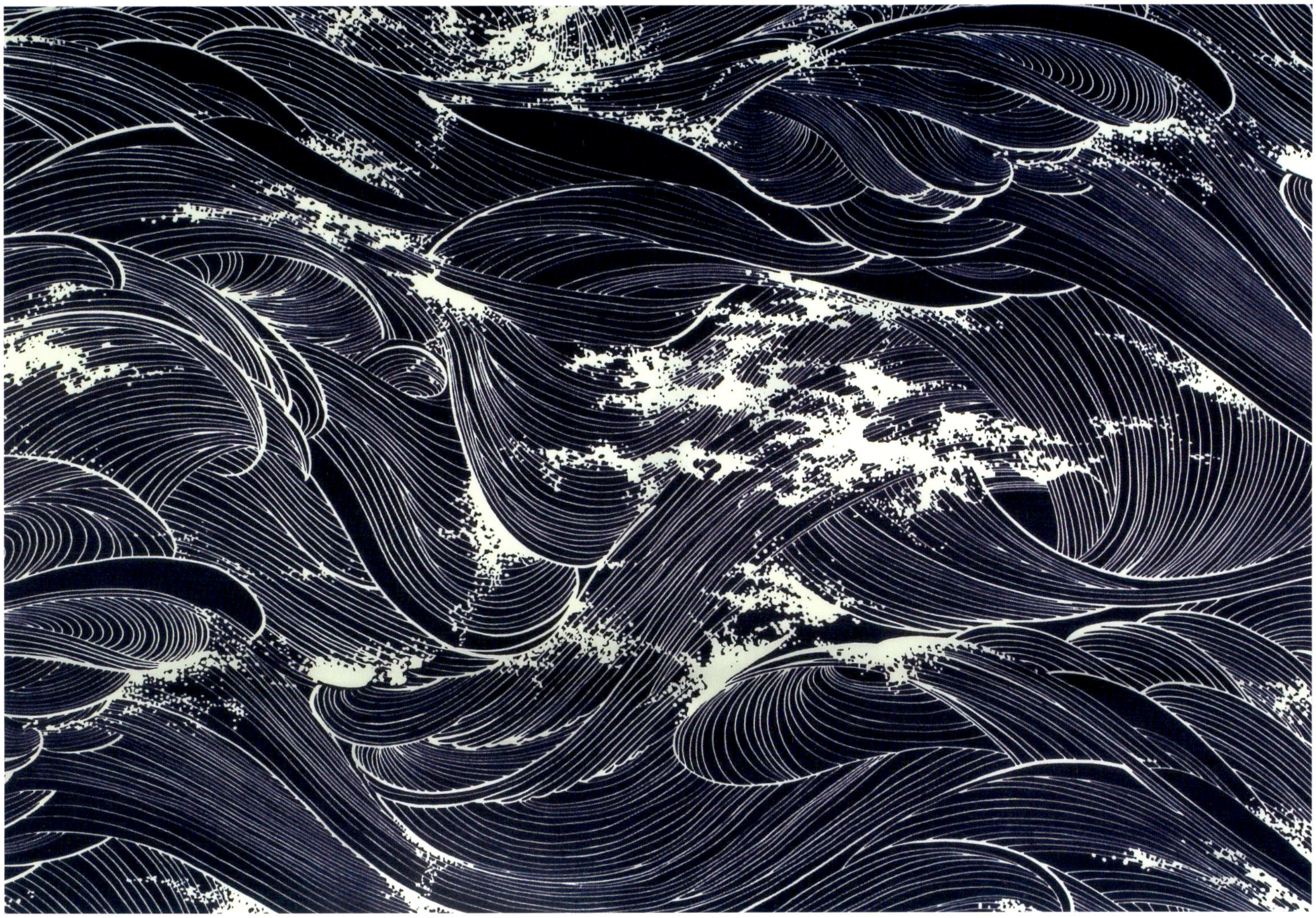

Kokeshi, in viscose, below, and Hang Glider, a border print in cotton broadcloth, bottom, are early examples of engineered prints and among the tens of thousands of archived Tori Richard prints.

Kim Scoggins
former vice president and chief operating officer of Tori Richard and present vice president of the Retail Services Group, Colliers Monroe Friedlander

"No one in the apparel industry had an eye for prints like Mort did. He would focus on an element. We'd walk along the back streets of Kyoto, Japan, into little studios that carried fabrics, art, or antiques. From across the room, he'd see something. It could be an obi sash, a vase, part of a Japanese screen, or a piece of art that was framed. It could have been a piece of a carpet. He had this gift of seeing what would work. He'd say, 'Wow, that really is something we can use.'

"And when he went to places like Lyon and Paris and different parts of Italy, he would select artwork with an eye that was unparalleled. He had a taste level in design that you can't teach. It's very difficult to find people who have a taste level like that, who can guide you, who know product creation, product development, and the over-all image that works in the design."

equipment for handling silk, for cutting and sewing silk on a large scale, simply does not exist in Hawai'i or in the U.S., and to my knowledge, it never has," explained Feldman.

In 1996, the Feldmans made the painful decision to close the Honolulu factory with its 70 seamstresses. "There were three reasons for this," Feldman continued. "First, we had quality problems. The equipment was antiquated, and there was no new labor coming into the market. I knew we had to upgrade the quality to where it was when my father was in the business, before he retired."

The infrastructure and labor force in existence at the time would not allow such improvement, he said. "Second, our worker's comp rates had exploded. In one year, they more than doubled. We would be out of business today if we tried to keep that factory. Third, we didn't have enough capacity. We were starting to solicit the better stores and customers to whom we used to sell. We simply could not produce enough units at the quality levels these stores expected and still keep production in Honolulu."

According to Feldman, "The pop-culture notion that companies move production overseas because it is less expensive is simply a myth

These recent engineered prints celebrate a joyful lifestyle, as in Hammock Man, *top;* Woody, *middle; and* Who Dat, *bottom.*

for us. In some ways, offshore production actually costs us more money." Considering China's thousands of years of weaving, printing and handling silk fabric, and then cutting it into intricate garments, he noted, "You realize that it's a skill that doesn't exist domestically."

What does exist is a good measure of creativity and skill in the execution of big ideas. Donna Burns, an Island artist and former designer for Tori Richard, feels that the strength of the company, while residing in its prints, is firmly grounded in art. "Mort always liked the very abstract painterly look," she noted. "There were always a couple of those in the line, no matter what. And there was a tightly patterned quality, almost Islamic, that ended up on the cotton lawns. And there were the wild abstract prints that Mort loved.

"He had a certain look, with flashes of color—reds, oranges, bright blues—and then a series of tight motifs, all at the same time. There was always a bright design, something Asian-inspired, something Islamic looking, and—what I call Amy Renshaw's forte—a unique juxtaposition of elements. That would be, say, a fabric design inspired by France, with a fleur-de-lis, to which Amy would add a monstera leaf—a painterly background, but with identifiable motif patterns."

While prints run the show, Tori Richard fabrications run the gamut, from knits and sleek cottons to silks in myriad weaves and weights. Embroidery is top-drawer, in bold engineered designs that form the centerpiece of the shirt. Luxurious silk jacquards have subtle leaf motifs woven into the fabrics like exotic shadows. Floating voiles and chiffons evoke nostalgia with a new twist. Silk interlock drapes and hugs at once. Colors jump and soothe.

When the design and manufacturing are completed, orders are shipped to some 2,500 better stores and specialty stores in all fifty U.S. states and throughout Asia, Europe, and the Caribbean. Thus does Mort Feldman's vision still travel throughout the world.

Top drawer: The uppermost drawer of the dresser, reserved for things of highest value, rank, or quality; residing in a premier position. Of the highest standards; excellent, as in "I wonder if Elroy would love this as much as I do," she reflected, feeling the sumptuous silk dress. *"It is so top drawer."*

In the Tori Richard offices on the outskirts of downtown Honolulu, a cadre of artists, designers, merchandisers, sales people, production staff, seamstresses, packers, and shippers hums away at the daily business of dressing people. The creative team huddles over the artwork, pondering colors and print potential. The designers and merchandisers build shape and form around the two dimensions of textile. The sales staff prognosticates, their finely honed fashion noses to the wind, always living a season or two ahead of real time.

Top Drawer

Patio, from 1997, with its matched front and border print, is popular among movie stars and has appeared on the large

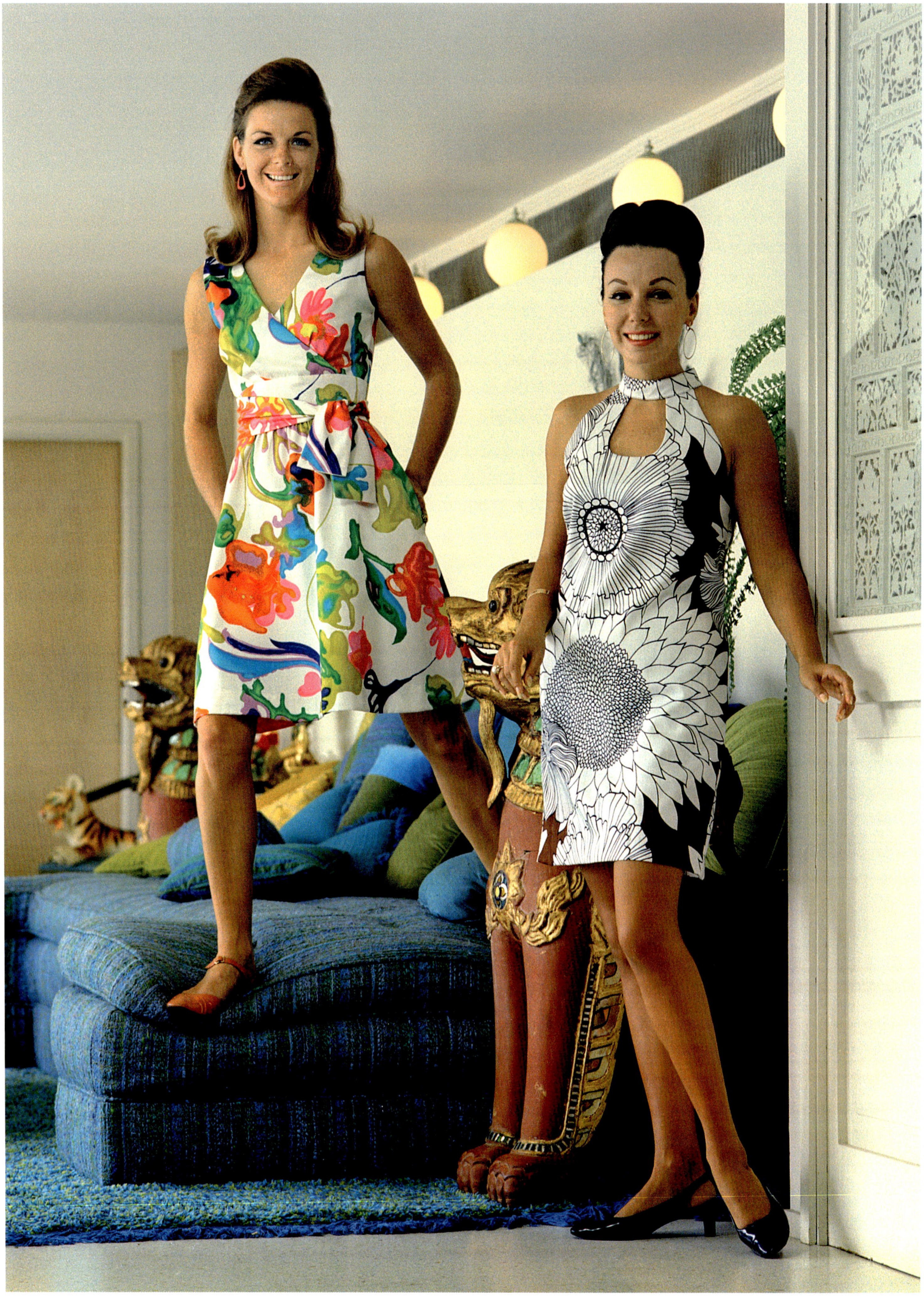

Top Drawer

Preceding page and below: Tori Richard vintage dresses represent several decades of courageous prints and superior print quality. Bottom right: The Cotton Producers Institute used Tori Richard in this Vogue advertisement in 1970.

Behind the scenes, in Honolulu and Asia, diligent seamstresses, tailors, artisans, and crafters are the invisible arbiters of Tori Richard quality, tending to the minutiae of buttons, seams, pockets, collars, and the finest particulars of garment construction. These details are significant, adding up to over-all excellence in the final product. Behind the broad strokes of high-profile prints and stylish, sophisticated design, the identity of Tori Richard is anchored as much in the fine points of construction as in the broad visual drama that meets the viewer's eye.

From start to finish, each step is driven by a historical obsession with quality and attention to detail that fuel the execution of a design.

"One of the things that distinguished Tori Richard from the beginning was my father's ability to spot any little imperfection in the garment, in every little detail," notes Jerry Feldman, Mort Feldman's son, who managed the Tori Richard New York showroom in the early 1980s. "I know that one of the things that made Tori Richard such a great success was my father's eye. He was a visual perfectionist who would see things in the garments that no one else would notice—not the designer, not the pattern maker, not the salesperson, not anyone.

"He would see things about the fit or something about the look that wasn't right, and invariably he was correct. If they'd go back and check, they'd always find that one sleeve was an iota longer, or something wasn't right. One of the reasons why Tori Richard is such a good clothing company is that he had an obsession to create the perfect garment in every way, in color, style, and detail."

He was also a stickler for color. June Feldman recalls the unrelenting, uncompromising standards her former husband applied to color. "The print would come back, and Mort would just sit there," she remembers. "We could sit there for a hundred hours with the color tabs going, reviewing and critiquing colors. I'd have it done, and Mort would say, 'That's the wrong shade of gray. It's too blue. There needs to be more brown….'"

Jerry Feldman, too, has vivid recollections of the time spent in "trying to get the colors right. We could spend the whole day working with the colors, making a single print work perfectly."

To the rigors of this kind of training, Josh Feldman, Mort's younger son, adds the gravitas of his art background and his own highly developed aesthetic. He has also

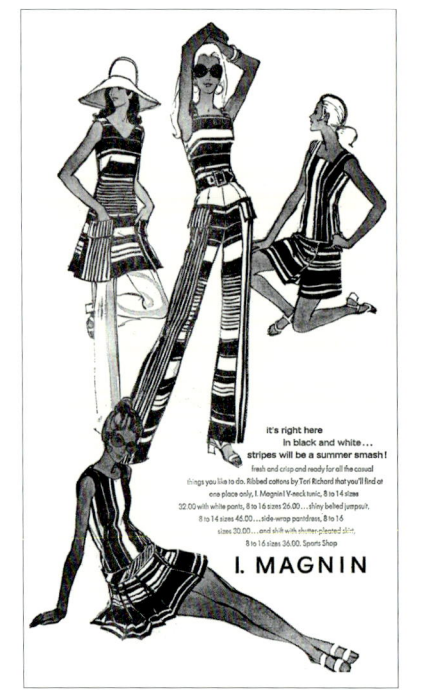

Tori Richard culottes were a hit, nationally advertised by I. Magnin and other prominent retailers, in the heyday of loungewear, the 1960s and '70s

Ellie Yamada
production manager

"Even if Mr. Feldman didn't agree with what you said, at least he listened. He didn't isolate himself from the employees. And he had a terrific sense of humor. When I reached 30 years here, I went and got a box of Godiva chocolates, because he liked chocolates. I said to him, 'Thanks for employing me for 30 years.' He said, 'You've been here for 30 years? That's longer than I've ever been married!'"

adopted a hands-on approach to the business that has surprised and impressed his employees.

"When Mort asked Josh to come home and help run the company, Josh had just graduated from the University of California at San Diego (UCSD) and was planning to go to law school," recalls Don MacRae, Tori Richard's Hawai'i sales rep. "I guess he agreed that he would come here for one year. He's still here.

"When he first came back, he jumped in and wanted to learn everything. He even wanted to learn how to sew, so he tried his hand at sewing a shirt on the equipment that we had in-house. He wanted to see how things worked and what the people were doing. He wanted to learn all the aspects of the business. He knew that if you're going to be involved in the construction and styling of a shirt, it's good to know how it goes together, to see how the pieces are supposed to fit."

The company was founded on a commitment as much to detail as to the colorful prints and high style that have made fashion headlines for decades. Eighty-four-year-old Mitsue Aka, retired pattern-maker and one of the three original partners in the company, says the engineered prints, one of Tori Richard's lasting signatures, reveal

Bottom: *Frances Kawamoto, merchandising assistant, has worked at Tori Richard since 1968.*
Below: *Cotton shifts were in vogue in the 1960s and '70s, when colors and prints had a Carnaby-Street spirit.*
Below right: *A trade publication advertisement series announces a seasonal line release.*

the lengths the company would go to in the creation of a quality item. The engineered print, usually a large tableau, is like a painting on the garment, calling for a specific kind of architecture to showcase the image. Patterns are usually not repeated, and the seams are matched to keep the image unbroken and the lines intact.

"I remember the engineered prints," recalls Aka. "It was hard to know how to lay them, how to mark them, so I would use spikes to hold the pattern in place. There were layers, and it was hard to keep them in the same position.

"The prints were big. Working around that, we had to waste a lot of material. Instead of three yards, we used four yards. Oh, but they were popular."

Kim Scoggins, former vice president and COO of the company, says that such refinements require special—and expensive—equipment. "At that time ('70s and '80s), it cost probably $25,000 to buy a machine that matched the pockets. Our garments were higher priced because of the fabrics we used, and because of the R and D (research and development) that went into the prints.

"But Mort was very cognizant of value. He was one of the best merchants I've ever worked with,

Mort Feldman with two of his signature influences: Japanese art, as in the screen behind him, and the matched-front Asian-printed shirt he wears, a Tori Richard phenomenon in the 1970s and '80s.

Jerry Chong
photographer

"Sometimes I used to print photos all night—fashion, real estate, Mort's personal property for insurance purposes. He used to tell me how he got started, how he was so poor that he used to go to the McInerny dumpster to collect old boxes to ship things. He always looked rich, no matter what, and he always had this sly grin, so you didn't know if he ate the canary or not.

"He was such a ritzy guy. He had such class and was very generous with his employees. At the Tori Richard parties at the Kahala Hilton, he used to give away trips to the mainland, pearl necklaces, and television sets. I was always overwhelmed by Tori Richard. Of all the companies I worked for, it was the most impressive. It was the way he treated his employees."

Pit Mechanic's Jump-Glorified
Shirt-shaped jump in knockout white sculptured cotton, medallion-patterned and deliciously bodied. Fits great on 6, 8, 10 or 12s. $50. Please add 85¢ beyond our delivery area. Miss Bergdorf At-Home Collections, Second Floor

BERGDORF GOODMAN
FIFTH AVENUE, 57 TO 58TH STREETS
ON THE PLAZA
NEW YORK 10019
PLAZA 2-7300

and a merchant can create value. For example, when you look at a woman's garment and notice, 'That's poorly made,' or 'That's really well made,' you're looking at the different elements, the image, the environment, the workmanship, and the actual materials that went into the sewing of that garment."

Ellie Yamada, Tori Richard's production manager and a long-time employee, knows more than most what goes into the execution of a Tori Richard design. Matched pockets may be an industry standard now, but there was a time when Tori Richard was one of the few companies that matched the pockets on men's shirts to keep the print unbroken and intact.

Matched fronts, in which the discrete integrity of the design continues across the two halves of a shirt front, remain a Tori Richard signature, a notable accomplishment in the apparel industry. "We have always been print-driven," continues Ellie Yamada. "We do a lot of matched fronts on shirts and on specific prints. From cars to cocktails and scenic images, we go the extra step to have matched fronts on engineered shirts."

When Josh came into the company, Tori Richard introduced matched fronts in 1994, and many other companies followed suit. "A

Vintage Tori Richard women's wear, from nautical white in cotton herringbone to playful patterns and prints, sets the tone for summer

lot of fabric can be wasted to assure a matched front," explains Donna Burns, a former designer for Tori Richard. "Within a given 'repeat,' a matched front means the pattern front and left must match exactly after being sewn. This is a very complex process, with even more fabric potentially wasted."

"Placement" and "mirrored" prints are other complicated Tori Richard features. "In the placement prints, the repeat needs to be done in such a way as to fit in the artwork presented on the back," continues Burns. "In some cases, the designs are mirrored on the front, which adds even more complexity."

As Yamada points out, care and attention are also devoted to the closures and fasteners of each garment. "We also match the buttons to the background of the garment; if the garment is reddish, the button is also reddish." Buttons carry a discreet Tori Richard logo, and on select styles, authentic shell buttons are used.

In men's shirts especially, where fashions change only subtly from one season to the next, there is considerable investment in the finer points that determine the crispness or drape of the garment. "When we pick the fabrication, we do a lot of research on interlining," Yamada continues. "We experiment with the

Printing screens await their colors, below, while Josh Feldman, below right, inspects embroidery in China.

Agatha Karpowicz, Tori Richard merchandiser since 1996, currently works with women's prints and the Harley Davidson licensed products.

different weights of interlining to find the one that best brings out the crispness of the garment." Because "a drooping collar is not very attractive," she adds, Tori Richard shirts contain collar stands—thin bands that connect the collar to the body of the shirt—that are supported by the selected interlining.

"Look at some other companies' shirts and feel the collars," says Yamada. "Sometimes you can feel three separate pieces, or layers. But with Tori Richard, you can only feel two, because we fuse the interlining to the top." The weight of the garment and the type of fabric—cotton lawn, rayon, cotton, and cotton blends—determine what type of interlining will be used. These special considerations are significant enhancements to the garment and are applied equally, when relevant, to women's apparel. French seams, sewn flat with raw edges turned in, offer a clean, crisp finish to each completed piece.

When skyrocketing costs and Mort's "retirement" called for a retrenching of the business, Ellie Yamada spent an inordinate amount of time finding and observing, for quality control, the people who would sew for the company under contract. "I was

Hand-painted, one-of-a-kind Tegaki prints, below, were produced and sold to great acclaim in the 1970s.

very, very picky," she explains. "I went all over the island to see these different people and evaluate their work. I spent time. I wanted to see not samples, but actual garments coming off the floor." She settled on just under half of the people she considered. "It took a solid year before I could say they were OK to sew our clothes," she says.

Those who knew Mort Feldman would not expect anything less. It took talent, determination, and no small measure of spunk to start a business like Tori Richard. Mort Feldman, Janice Moody and Mitsue Aka, the three original partners, possessed those qualities in spades, but the real test of their synergy was to come. Only time would tell if longevity would follow the initial blush of acceptance and seal Tori Richard's fate as a manufacturer of lasting repute. Only time would tell if Tori Richard would stay *top drawer*.

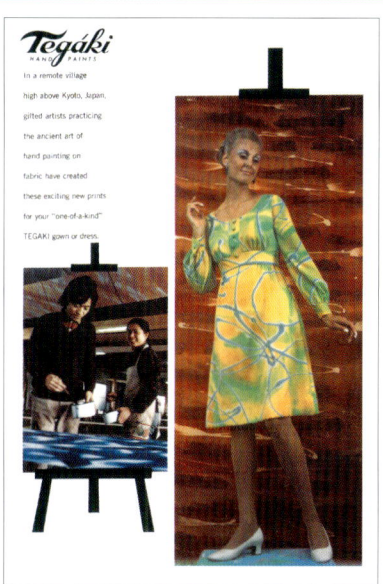

"I did it! I did it! I found some brand new, absolutely gorgeous summer fun clothes for women!" raved the *Vancouver Sun* of March 25, 1966. "They're youthful but not childish. They are something your 16-year-old daughter isn't going to beg, borrow or steal… And they have never been in Canada before. Designed by Tori Richard of Honolulu, these sun clothes have all the enchantment and color of Hawaii but without the stereotyped Hawaiian muu-muu look."[1]

Tori Glory

Style File

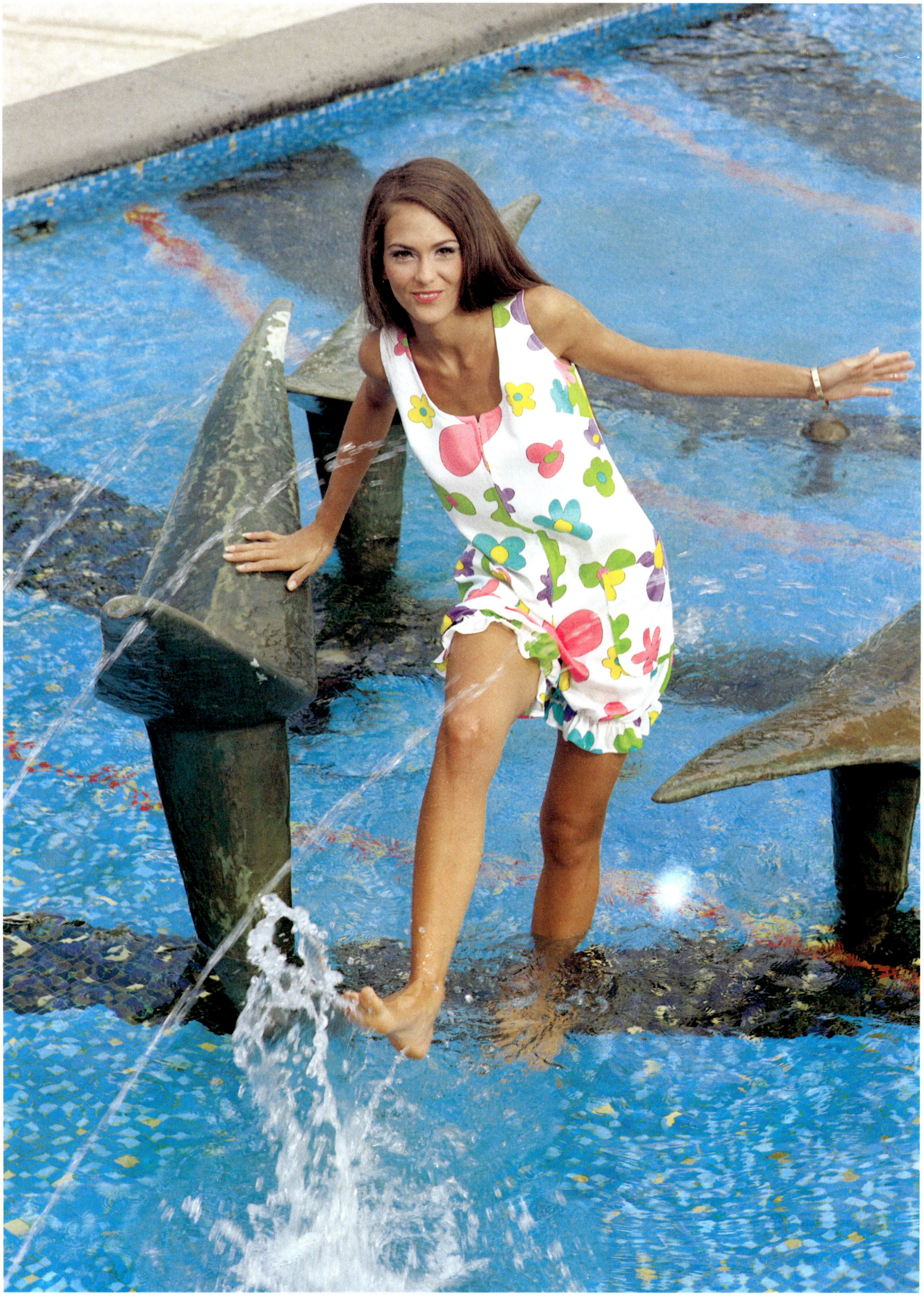

Tori Glory

Women's fashion has always been at the heart of Tori Richard. From the first fashion riffs to roll off the mind of inaugural designer Janice Moody, Tori Richard has centered on the feminine form—as a backdrop for its prints, as the Muse for its art, as a vehicle for fun, and as the messenger of its aesthetic statement. Dramatic loungewear, head-turning swimsuits, tunic outfits, form-fitting sheaths, Asian-inspired dresses, cocktail fantasies, floor-skimming skirts, around-the-clock, go-anywhere apparel, even matching leggings—Tori Richard women's wear made a strong fashion statement long before men's wear claimed its share of the spotlight in the 1970s.

But over five decades, Tori Richard's glory days have spanned both sides of the gender aisle. Focusing on its prints and the quality of its design and manufacture, Tori Richard has dressed women and men in topnotch fabrics and an understated, enduring ease. From the leisurely primness of the late 1950s, to the freewheeling '60s and its Carnaby Street palette, to the growing sophistication of the succeeding decades, Tori Richard has surfed the tides of fashion while staying true to its aesthetic roots.

Preceding page: *National advertisements in the 1970s featured chic women's wear for many occasions.* Below: *playwear in the 1960s.*

"I don't think my father ever imagined that the company would be as successful as it is today," reflects Josh Feldman at the threshold of his company's next half-century. "I'm fascinated by the company in the 1960s. It was supposedly the golden era. You can see it in the archives, in the Tori Richard ads for prestigious stores like Saks Fifth Avenue, Bergdorf Goodman, and I. Magnin. It was an energetic, exciting era.

"And I think we've eclipsed that. It's a much bigger world now, so the sense of success is different. But in terms of the sheer number of units going out the door, we've surpassed everything that we've ever done."

That comment speaks volumes, because there was a time when Tori Richard enjoyed a reputation as Hawai'i's top fashion house. Tori Richard's buoyant style in women's wear enlivened Fifth Avenue windows, advertisements and editorial space in the top publications of the country. Fashion editors fell in love with Janice Feldman's splashy style, and the collection soared through the sixties.

"Down among the sheltering palms, our made-in-Hawaii exclusive," reads a 1962 Saks Fifth Avenue advertisement for Janice Feldman's line of Tori Richard swimwear and "cabana clothes." Summer shifts and "swim shapes" were fashioned at the time in ocean, fruit, and garden colors, with Mandarin collars and Moorish prints in fabrics named Arnel®, Dacron®, Polyplush, "tree bark fabric," polished cotton, sharkskin, cotton surah, "Maharani silk," and a plethora of others, reflecting the country's fascination with textiles old and new.

Prints had names like Picasso, Crescendo, Roma, Happiness, Montego, Gaiety, Lido, Hampton, Pacifica, Rio, Horizon, Daisy-Mae, Arabesque, and endlessly creative monikers from around the world. Styles were dubbed "cocktail shorty," "toga mu'u," and "Tori Taper," and were "deliciously bodied"[2] and "confidently elegant."[3] Whether in black-and-white or a riot of color, poncho pants and harem pants were "dramatic little get-ups" for reveling in leisure and launching quiet evenings at home. While well-dressed women entertained at home in their Tori Richard loungewear, they also dressed formally in their Tori Richard dresses.

"When I first moved to Hawai'i, you could go to the Honolulu Symphony and see a woman dressed in one of those engineered-print dresses with a fur stole wrapped around her," recalls June Feldman, former merchandise

Cotton was king in the 1960s, and pink was the color of the times.

Below right: Piazza, a simple 1960s dress with jacket, proves that style is timeless.

stylist for the company. "Back then in Honolulu, that was the epitome of being elegant and dressed up."

Casual fashions were the other side of the coin, and equally popular. "Pressed for time? Catch Tori Richard's non-stop knits that are pressed for life!" quipped a Liberty House ad in the late 1960s. Natural fibers had equal say, in witty ads such as the nationwide campaign of the National Cotton Council in 1968: "Tori Richard is using a famous fabric that has an age-old pedigree, sometimes goes wild, but always acts civilized. It's fresh, cool, comfortable cotton, seen here as audacious as Tori Richard wants it. The March issue of *Mademoiselle* will show it in full color."

In the 1970s, Tori Richard opened its second New York showroom for its burgeoning loungewear line. June Feldman had introduced that line, an idea that proved to be remarkably fertile, a mother-lode of future successes. Many of the most dramatic prints of that era were large, body-covering designs, engineered prints, which determined the architecture of the garment. Each was a feat of technical precision and visual mastery. The high drama of the engineered print, responsible for much of the buzz of Tori Richard's glory days, had its genesis in loungewear.

"We would find those designs in Europe," recalls June Feldman. "It

Mitsue Aka, bottom left in a casual moment while on business in Hong Kong, was one of the three original founders of Tori Richard. Below, Mort Feldman meets with Aka, right, and Frances Shimazu, left, in 1970. Bottom right: Tori Richard in a national ad campaign in Vogue magazine, by the Cotton Producers Institute.

would be a small image of an elephant, for example, and we'd say, 'We can make this bigger.' So we'd send it to Japan and ask them to enlarge it by 50 percent, or 100 percent, or whatever looked best. Mort was very precise about it and would do things like move the elephant's foot by an inch, to keep with the scale and proportion."

Years later, as the loungewear trend was cresting, another concept, this time for men, was incubating, a glimmer in the designer's eye. While loungewear had been based on large, dramatic prints, the new men's shirt was based on its opposite: a print with a tight repeat. "We were in Europe, and I picked up a Liberty of London shirt," June Feldman remembers. "They had little florals, and I thought they were interesting. The market was changing; loungewear was not such a big product anymore, and I had the idea of doing little necktie prints on cotton. Mort found the lawn (a fine Egyptian cotton), and it took off."

Cotton lawn shirts, with their patented Tori Richard finish, have remained a company staple, a perpetual trophy from the glory days. The fabric has remained in the line for nearly a quarter century. It was only natural that Josh would bring back the engineered print after seeing the newfound success of

Douglass Smoyer
owner of Retail Strategies and former Tori Richard general manager

"I got mad at Mort for the way he sometimes treated people. I had worked with him for about seven years, and one day I just said, 'I will not go through the rest of my life listening to him.' I went to the Waikīkī Yacht Club, went on my boat about 20 miles offshore with a very expensive bottle of red wine, opened the wine, drank it, and said, 'Good-bye Mort.' That's how we ran the business—very emotional.

"But I have to tell you, whatever taste and creativity I have in the world of apparel came from Mort Feldman. He was my teacher. I'll always be indebted to him for what he taught me. I never could have run all those stores without the taste level that he instilled in me. He gets the major credit."

---

the lawn in men's apparel.

"My father would always talk about these prints that he would run in the '60s in the women's line," explains Josh Feldman. "They were giant prints, sixty-inch repeats that would run the length of the garment. The dresses had a bold print that would run from the bottom all the way up to the top. I kept looking at that and wondering, is there an equivalent of that in men's shirts?"

The epiphany came in 1995, when Feldman was in a vintage clothing store in Sacramento, California. "There used to be a company named Nik-Nik, which isn't around anymore," he explains. "And I ran across this Nik-Nik shirt of a giant tennis player, a huge motif across the shirt, with a matching front. And it hit me: This is what Tori Richard was doing in women's wear. And this is what we could do in men's." The revelation re-introduced the Tori Richard engineered print, this time for men's wear, and is today a technique that is widely imitated throughout the industry. Individually made, requiring twice as much fabric—four yards—as the typical shirt, the Tori Richard engineered print remains an industry hallmark.

Translated into the current fashion vocabulary, the Tori Richard engineered print could be a large embroidered motif on a silk shirt, or printed foliage at the bottom of a silk surah skirt. Diaphanous silk chiffon is also a worthy canvas, in tunics, pants, and sun dresses, with a nod to Art Nouveau in a print named Arabesque.

Collections that are not engineered roam the world and the seasons, too, with names like Falling Leaves, Rococo, Kenya and Sand Garden, in colors, fabrics, and styles that live up to the go-anywhere, anytime Tori Richard standard. Shirts, skirts, jackets, trench coats, sweaters, sun dresses, camisoles, trimmer long-sleeved men's shirts, coordinated trousers and shorts— the collections come alive in fabrics like silk interlock, jersey, denim, knits, luxurious silk blends, and state-of-the art fabrications like Tencel® and its blends.

The Tori Richard print archive is nearly 20,000 strong, growing yearly by the hundreds. Underscoring every square inch of the archive is the Feldman family legacy. "The mission, since my dad and I came back to the company, was to restore the company's legacy, which is the better end of the market for men's and women's resort wear," explains Josh Feldman. "So at Tori Richard today, we continue to move forward while we honor where we started."

Necklines, waistlines, and assertive prints figure prominently in vintage Tori Richard women's wear, below.

Doreen Kapuakela
shipping clerk

"I've been here 35 years, a shipping clerk from the beginning. I've been to 35 Christmas parties—at the Halekulani, Kahala Hilton, and other nice places. When I started, I thought Mr. Feldman was so mean to me. He came over and said, 'That's not right.' He didn't know I was new. An hour later, he wrote me a sorry note. From that time on, I really loved him. He was such a good boss, like a father to me.

"He taught me to work hard, that your job is important. There were other packers, and I had a lot of compliments on the way I packed. My job was important. We've had bad times and good times, but no one was laid off. He liked to go to every department to see how we were doing. If we weren't doing it right, he could yell. He could be a teaser, too. He had a mean temper but also a great sense of humor. He was like a father figure to me all those years. Maybe that's why I've lasted this long."

Zenzational

Like the rays of the rising sun, the Asian influence on Tori Richard is wide ranging and profound. A Chinese moon gate greets the visitor to the Tori Richard Waikīkī Beach store. Japanese cranes and calligraphic brush strokes swoop across timeless silk shirts with the Tori Richard label. Elegant swirls of koi, the Japanese carp, add grace and movement to men's shirts, reappearing through the decades in new and modernized forms. Mandarin collars, Chinese frog closures, and kimono-inspired sleeves are Tori Richard classics, updated and freshened to meet emerging tastes.

Torigami

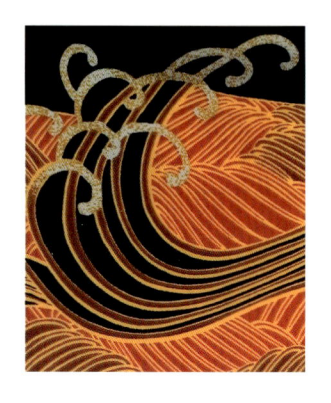

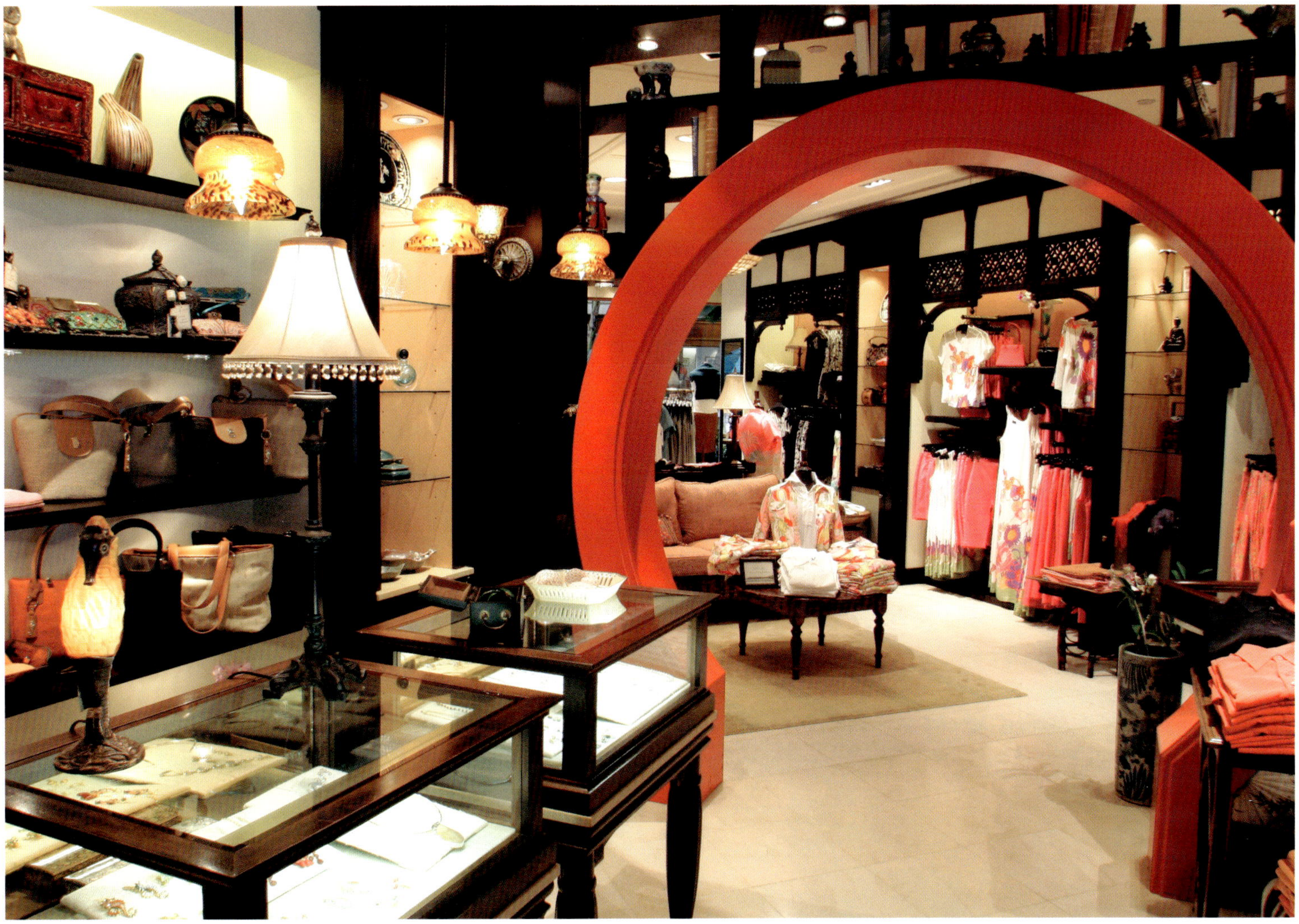

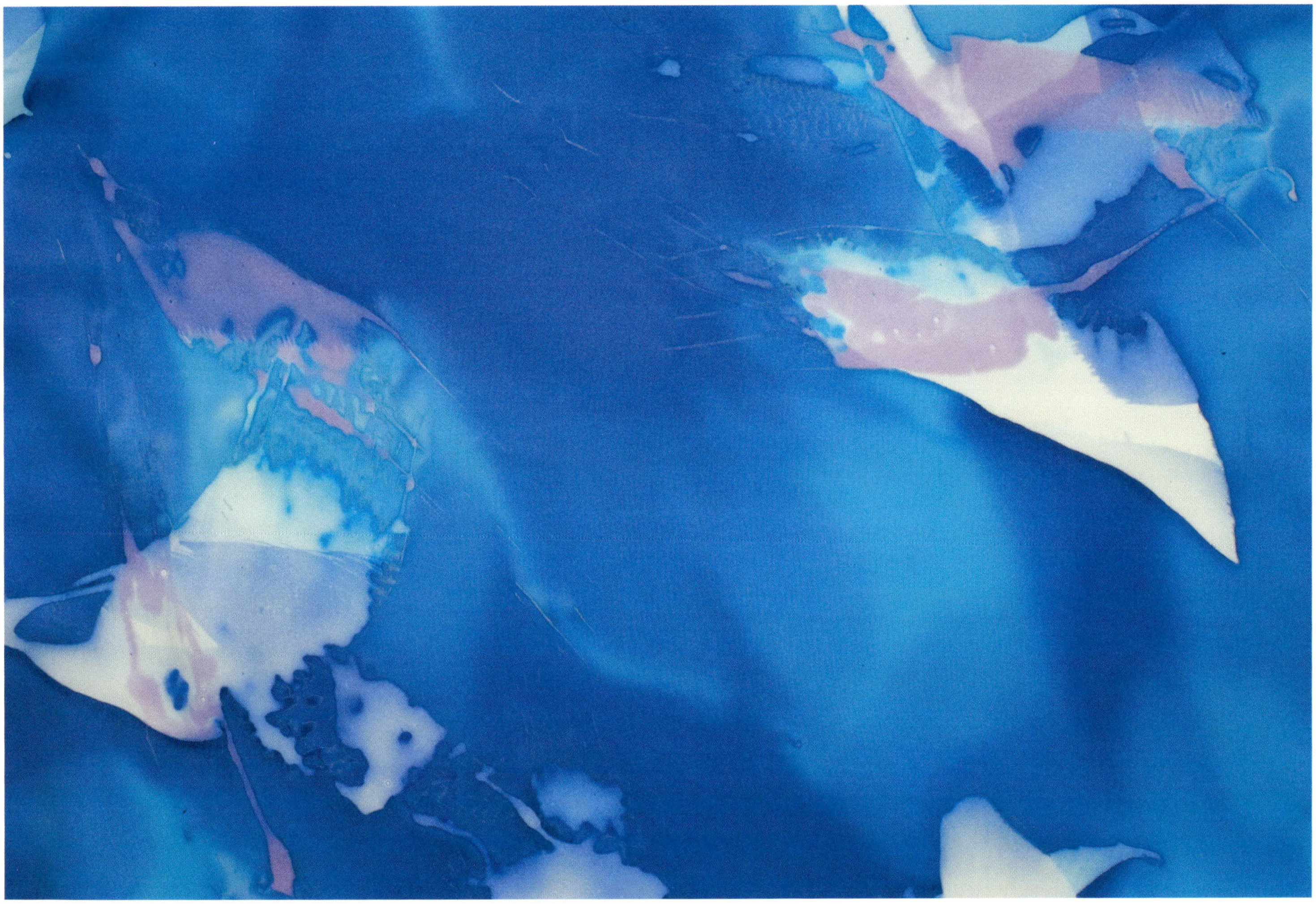

Torigami

Preceding page: The Chinese moon gate and Japanese one-of-a-kind Tegaki prints are Asian influences, as is Shangri La, the brocade coat above, and Yume ("dream" in Japanese), right.

At the company's Honolulu headquarters, Asian prints and monikers fill the archives, and Asian influences, from statues to paintings to Japanese screens, accent the offices and showroom. Across the ocean, in Japan and China, printers and textile mills use cutting-edge technologies to imbue their raw goods with the ultimate in quality for Tori Richard products. In print and environment, temple lions, Buddha statues, torii gates, and Japanese screens are Tori Richard design elements. From the architecture of its stores to the technology of its printing to the aesthetics of its designs, Tori Richard's visual identity mines the beauties and traditions of the East.

Founder Mort Feldman's fascination with Asia is built into the company's core, its cultural DNA. Even before his fashion line was developed, Feldman was importing "Tori Tops" from Japan and selling them with a partner at the International Market Place in Waikīkī. Based on the gift-wrapping fabric used in Japan as *furoshiki*, they were "rayon squares, basically scarves, stitched at the shoulder and at the armholes, so they hung down as little tops," recalls Diana Snyder, a former fashion model who met

Summer 2005 highlighted Fiesta, in holiday colors and sumptuous silk georgette with mother-of-pearl buttons.

Feldman in California and moved to Hawai'i at his urging. "They were printed with cherry blossoms and had a strong Japanese influence. They were very, very popular."

Those tops were among the first minuscule, commercial, embryonic expressions of Feldman's passion for things Japanese. Having reached its peak before and just following World War II, waning and then spiking after 1945, Japanese art was the rage in Europe by the time Tori Richard was established in the mid-1950s. Fueling the trend, major exhibitions in Paris and London unseated surrealism, Cubism, and other abstract art from the hearts and minds of many collectors and replaced them with a yen for Japanese art. But with his deep and longstanding love of Japanese cuisine, antiques, and art, and his understanding of the cohesive aesthetic underlying them, Mort Feldman transcended these trends. Now in its second generation, even while Mediterranean, African, and other ethnic elements claim their share of the stage, the Asian aesthetic heritage remains in the spotlight at Tori Richard.

According to Josh, the CEO and younger Feldman, "We apply what are essentially Japanese aesthetics to every single print we create. This standard was established by my

Symmetry and order, as in the dress below, and the serenity of a koi gliding through a lotus garden, as in Koi, bottom, are among the diverse applications of Asian aesthetics to Tori Richard designs.

father from day one. Space, proportion, harmony—these are the fundamental characteristics of any good Tori Richard print, whether of yesterday or today."

Some women's fashions bear crisply modernized Asian features, such as wrap dresses with obi (kimono sash) interpretations. Balancing its modernist, eclectic art styles, Tori Richard prints are populated also with bamboo, batik, and Balinese motifs, a nod to Southeast Asia. Like the distant vibration of a Kyoto temple bell or a fleeting tendril of exquisite incense, Japanese motifs and aesthetic refinements are a subtle yet palpable presence. In the world according to Feldman, winds from the Eastern horizon carry mysterious and exotic elements.

Japanese printers, the finest in the trade, were the first indication of the founding Feldman's depth of commitment. In the early days of Tori Richard, Mort Feldman broke a cartel by forging his own solid relationships with textile companies in Japan. Today those relationships are welded into Tori Richard culture, carried forward in an ongoing exchange of ideas and technology that extends to China—and even to Peru— as well. Japanese, Chinese, Thai, Indonesian, and Korean companies print and manufacture the Tori Richard fabrics. China is favored for some production due to its expertise in silk: Its centuries-old history with silk and the high quality of its workmanship make it increasingly viable as a Tori Richard partner, as has been the case for decades.

Still, the Japanese aesthetic is without peer in the company's ethnic *oeuvre*. With her husband, Janice Moody Feldman, the company's first designer, captured the look, proportions, and details of Japan with undeniable panache. Her patterns, silhouettes, shapes, and shades had fresh eye appeal in designs such as Zabuton, a geometric print from the late 1950s. Sold with matching zabutons, the print was styled in a hapi coat, swimsuit, "Shoji set" (pant suit), tea-timer (a long, slashed dress to wear over pants), and sun dress in orange and pink or orchid and blue cotton. Succeeding designers followed Moody's precedent. They peppered the showrooms and archives with prints named Furoshiki, Shibui, Lotus, Origami, Orientale, Kabuki, Cho-Cho, Tegaki, and dozens of other concepts.

In 1971, four years after Janice Moody left the company, the Tegaki line created a buzz that is still remembered in the industry. Japanese artists in Osaka, Japan, strung twelve-yard pieces of fabric between bamboo poles and painted them, by hand, in pairs. No two fabrics, and therefore no two garments, were alike. Each unique fabric took its place in Tori Richard history. Haruko Moberg, an award-winning designer and native of Japan, had apprenticed with Moody and was known for helping to coordinate that fashion first.

"The delicate hand-painted art is never duplicated," reads a Tori Richard Tegaki ad from the mid-1970s. "Gone forever the thought of seeing your friend or neighbor in the same dress."

Tegaki was an upscale product, painted on polyester "suede" that was 36 inches wide and held vibrant colors well. It was, remembers Kim Scoggins, former vice president and COO of the company, an artistic and technical feat that would have been, in terms of durability, difficult on cotton or silk. In technique and concept, Tegaki underscored the company's devotion to art, to artists, to the print.

"Tegaki had to be 36 inches wide because the artist couldn't reach across a 45-inch piece of fabric to paint," Scoggins explains. "We'd go to this little studio upstairs in an old wooden building. It was almost too primitive, it was so... *cottage industry*. We'd see the fabric stretched

Whirlpool, top, from the 1970s, and the monochrome of a stylized forest, above, bring Asian touches to Tori Richard textiles. Right, East and West unite in culottes and kimono-inspired sash from 1972.

A Mandarin collar and frog closures bring the Orient to life in a Tori Richard silk top from the late 1950s, left. Below, the shirt named Capri and a 1970s dress with kimono-inspired sleeves bow to Mort Feldman's love of Asia.

out, suspended in air. That allowed it to dry right after the artists painted it. We had very small runs to cut from, which made it expensive. We made long women's dresses, we made short women's dresses, we made shirts." The shirt, $36 at the time, would be "a $200 shirt today," he says. "It sold like hotcakes."

In 1979, a Tori Richard press release touted the gift-giving custom of Furoshiki, the square of fabric in which Japanese gifts are tied and bundled for presentation: "From the traditional Japanese custom of enclosing gifts in appropriate wrappings called *Furoshiki* (each telling something about the gift or the giver), comes a new concept in fashion tops and dresses," it read. It cited the fabric of spun rayon, "softer to the touch and a great feeling of luxury," in prints inspired by Nara, known for its bamboo forests, and Kyoto, "where autumns of yesterday and today endure."

A year later, when actor Richard Chamberlain and *Shogun* were fueling the sushi, kimono, and Japanese-culture craze in the Western world, the *Honolulu Star-Bulletin* ran this item in its "Dave Donnelly's Hawaii" column: "Besides capturing about 60 percent of the available television-viewing audience on the mainland, James Clavell's 'Shogun' has apparently worked its inscrutable magic on the fashion industry as well. Since the $22-million epic played on the mainland last week, Tori Richard has received huge orders for four of their women's loungewear Japanese prints from the likes of Neiman Marcus, Sakowitz, I. Magnin's and Bloomingdale's."[1]

The Asian aesthetic surpassed the individual designers who came and went at Tori Richard. Each period in the company's history has had its own Asian emblems, invented, adapted, re-created, and modernized to reflect contemporary tastes. In today's visual vocabulary of quiet, understated elegance, the language of *shibui* speaks volumes in the Tori Richard aesthetic. If *shibui* is a whisper, a quality of excellence that needs no amplification, it speaks classically and eloquently to the Tori Richard standard.

Former Tori Richard designer Haruko Moberg was a style force in the late '60s and early '70s.

The Tegaki shirt, far right, and floor-skimming dress, right, helped pave the way for the era of the rising sun.

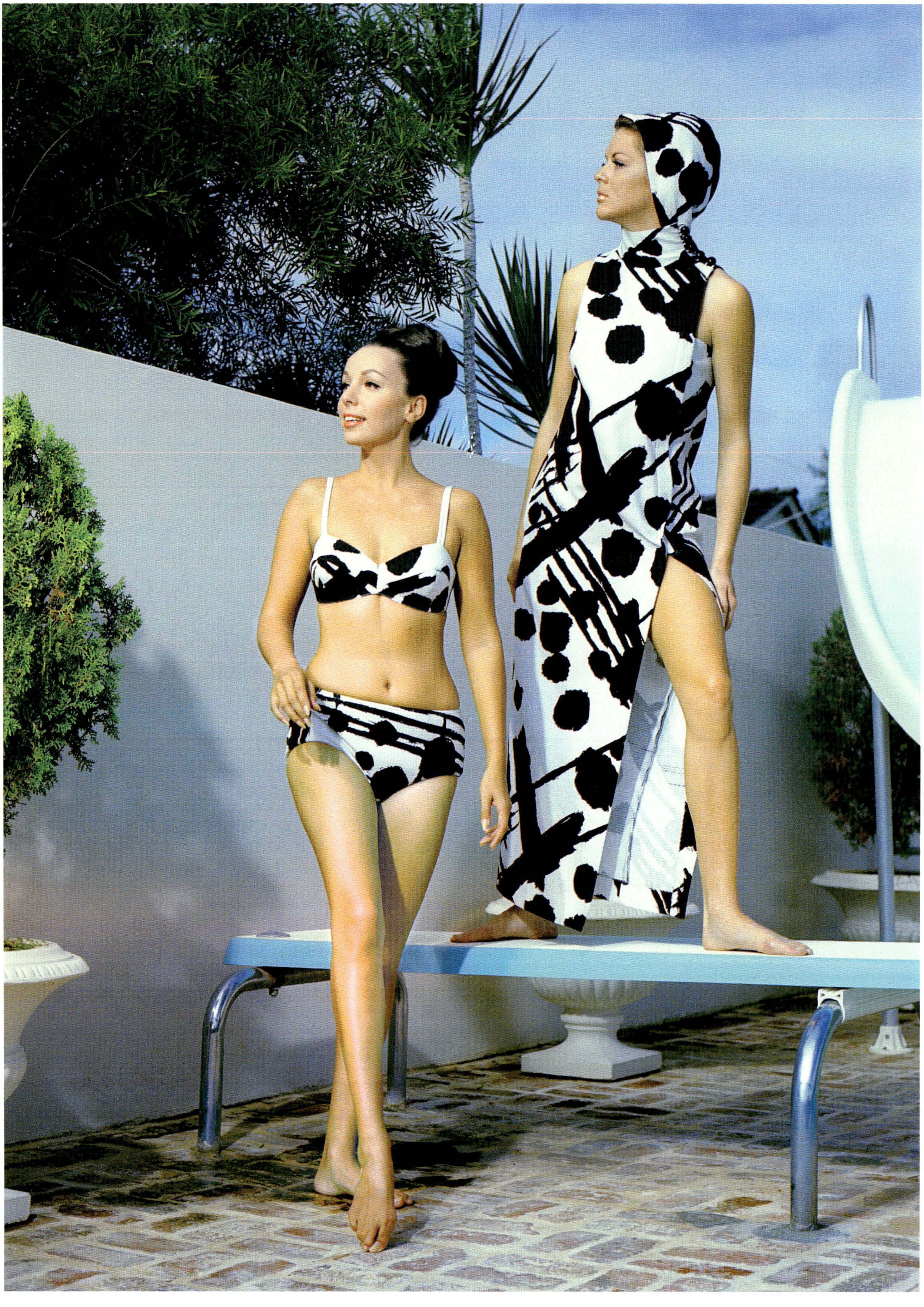

For all the whispers of elegance and understatement that define Tori Richard style, there is often a thread of drama woven into the apparel. Throughout its history, Tori Richard prints and designs have turned heads with their boldness and generated oceans of journalistic ink with their flamboyant, photogenic impact. Ruled by art, defined by quality, and timeless in their relevance, these designs sail through the seasons in all shapes, palettes, and textures.

The '60s had their large prints and bold engineered designs, emblazoned on the fabrics of the day. Stylized border prints accented willowy bodies.

Grand Entrance

poolside drama... the hooded shift in a bold play of black-on-white pique, by Tori Richard. 8 to 12 sizes 40.00

I. MAGNIN & CO

DESERT INN FASHION PLAZA • PALM SPRINGS
AND ALL OTHER I. MAGNIN STORES

■ REPRINTED FROM HARPER'S BAZAAR, FEBRUARY 1968

Grand Entrance

Geometrics were printed in long, full repeats. African animal prints suggested adventures afar and deep, primitive mysteries. Tribal totems and ethnic influences brought the far corners of the world into the Tori Richard look.

Bright colors and geometric patterns brought silky cottons, silks, and a spate of synthetics to life. Fabrics named sharkskin, Darnel®, Arnel®, and Dacron® absorbed the colors in fashions that went from the beach to evening. In one print, Imperial Screen, introduced in 1962, thirty-two screens were used to create an intricate, multi-layered design.

Skirts could be billowy, structured, or pencil thin, jumpsuits lean and leggy. Some shapes were vaguely triangular, like stylized inverted pyramids, broad at the shoulders and narrowing at the hips. High-end caftans, burnooses, djellabas, tent shifts, hostess gowns, and unique harem dresses made grand entrances everywhere, evoking Maharani splendor and Oriental luxury. During the day, sun dresses and swimsuits captured attention at the pool and beach, and after sunset, sleek, simple cocktail dresses were the backdrop for head-

Previous page: A February, 1968, advertisement in Harper's Bazaar.
Left: a vintage Tori Richard knit dress with tailored elements, paired with bold geometrics for a sense of surprise.

turning prints.

"Come to the big calypso cotton skirmish!" reads a 1966 Tori Richard ad. "Such a clash of head-on color—a surge of cotton on the loose. It's the big playdress uprising… Take your print hot blooded, helter skelter, or gentle as an island breeze."

In 1966, a print named Arabesque made a splashy début with its intricate, stylized paisley pattern that evoked images of peacock feathers in an Art Nouveau headpiece or on a Follies Bergère stage. The print proved timeless, as relevant in the 2006 collection as it was in decades past. Modernized in silk crinkle chiffon with cascade sleeves, Arabesque is a Tori Richard classic that can be adapted and interpreted for all times and many tastes.

In 1963, high drama hit the beaches in the "Ice Capades," a Tori Richard extravaganza that was red-hot in its sizzle. In its spring-summer collection, Tori Richard transported 4,500 pounds of ice to its Waikīkī photo shoot. It was the dead of winter for snow-bound mainlanders and a sunny paradise for Islanders, a contrast made for the fashion gods. Set against the backdrop of ice, bold colors played against white in bikinis, sun dresses, A-shaped shifts, beach

Timeless vintage: Tori Richard turns an ethnic motif into a two-piece pool ensemble with engineered print wrap skirt.

Tori Richard's "Ice Capades" fashion shoot in 1963 required 4,500 pounds of ice to be delivered to sunny Waikīkī. The spring-summer ad campaign appealed to snow-bound mainlanders in the dead of winter.

cover-ups, and the full array of sports wear. Fabrics were imported from Paris, West Germany, Switzerland, and the Netherlands, which sent woven denim featuring intricate, hand-screened florals.

"High fashion is hitting us right away now instead of months after a trend is introduced," Mort Feldman is quoted in a *Sunday Star-Bulletin and Advertiser* article from 1963. Added fashion editor Cleo Evans: "He may well have added that not only is this progressive Island firm hot on the heels of new high style in casual wear trends, but is very likely setting them as well."[1]

In its offshore fashion shows, Tori Richard was applauded in places like New York, Dallas, Los Angeles, and France. A showing in a Paris hotel received raves for styles named Galaxy, Razzmatazz, and Paravent, designed to make a grand entrance anywhere. In the spring of 1969, the *Dallas Times Herald* touted fashions from Tori Richard and Baba Kea, another Island designer, for projecting Hawai'i as "a fascinating state of mind and Hawaiian fashions as a vibrant influence that has achieved global status."[2] The clothing, the article continued, was "ticketed for play places anywhere, from Rio to the Riviera, from Mexico's Acapulco to Portugal's Algarve, from Palm Beach to Palm Springs."[3]

Polynesian prints were included, but "the new breed of prints will steal the spotlight with the charm of their stylized florals, sassy berries and crazy quilt teamings on couture-mannered textured cottons."[4] Though based in Hawai'i, Tori Richard created fashions that may have held Island influences, but could not be geographically confined or defined.

As in the 21st century, "lifestyle" was on everyone's lips in the 1970s, when designer Ralph Lauren designed his own boutiques and introduced the "lifestyle merchandising" concept in department stores. It was a new way to do one-stop shopping for the Polo brand.[5] "In 1970, Lauren convinced Bloomingdale's to put all his ties, suits, dress shirts, and raincoats together in his own special little boutique," writes Terri Agins in *The End of Fashion*.[6] The concept of coordinated fashions gained momentum nationally, and for small companies like Tori Richard, it validated ongoing design philosophies while it introduced new avenues of merchandising. From the beginning, Tori Richard fashions were an expression of gracious living in a time when entertaining, poolside leisure, cocktail parties—and simply looking chic—were a popular equivalent of the exclusive

A Japanese screen from Mort Feldman's collection serves as backdrop for a 1960s cotton sateen dress. Above left, Arabesque in its vintage form, reinterpreted for 2006 in a beaded silk tunic, above.

Designer Amos Kotomori featured bold, elemental knits in his Tori Richard collection, as in this strapless gown with kimono influences.

Polo message.

Tori Richard's sense of resort culture—in the exotic Pacific, with its tribal undertones and tapa prints—found new expression in the '70s, when cross-cultural currents swept East and West in rich juxtapositions. Tongan tapa prints and cutting-edge Polyplush fabrics, hot off the Japanese mills, contrasted traditions and technologies. Tori Richard showings in Hong Kong were enthusiastically received as sophisticated resort wear "suited for a leisurely cruise on a luxury liner or lounging around a pool or cocktail bar of some smart resort hotel," according to the *HongKong Standard*.[7] That collection included flowing caftans, simple jersey tops, the classic shirtwaist dress, "simple lines and rich colour," and black-and-white prints for added drama.

In the late 1970s, a young Japanese-American designer named Amos Kotomori knocked on the doors of fashion houses in Paris—and got in. Carrying his *furoshiki*, the Japanese fabric square tied around objects as a carrying vessel, Kotomori gained entrée to design houses like Ted Lapidus, Pierre Cardin, Christian Dior, and the Japanese phenomenon, Kansai Yamamoto. Upon his return to Hawai'i, says Kotomori, he designed a line of "convertible dresses"—

Amos Kotomori's convertible dresses from the late '70s and early '80s fuse East and West, flair and practicality.

dresses that could be worn in multiple styles—and proposed them to Mort Feldman at Tori Richard.

Kotomori's samples were simple black knits with polka dots and stripes, fashioned in stark architectural shapes that had a life of their own. It was an act of chutzpah, taking solid fabrics to a manufacturer renowned for its prints. But Kotomori ended up touring the mainland for Tori Richard—ten cities and fourteen shows in three weeks—and saw his line carried in stores like Sakowitz, Neiman Marcus, Saks Fifth Avenue, Marshall Field, and Nordstrom.

In the heart of winter in mainland cities, Kotomori's barefoot Tori Richard models wore slicked-back hair with orchids and anthuriums. There were no accessories. At the fashion shows, he maximized the drama by appearing as a ninja as he changed the models on stage. The twelve coordinates in bold jerseys, nine of them in one size, were a hit, and his collection, with its multiple looks and possibilities, from tunics and pants to sashed dresses and drapey skirts, garnered awards for Tori Richard. In 1980, Kotomori was named "Designer of the Year" at the Hawaiian Fashion Guild's first annual fashion awards banquet.

"Mort wanted prints, but I wanted solids, and in special colors

Amos Kotomori
award-winning designer for Tori Richard in the early 1980s

"When I returned from Paris in 1979, I decided to make a line of clothes, simple black-and-white knits with polka dots and stripes. The idea was convertible clothing: one garment that could be re-fashioned into multiple styles—a line of convertible dresses. I wrapped my designs in my *furoshiki* and took them to Tori Richard. As Bobbie Taum was about to give me an appointment with Mort, out he walked from his office.

"Tori Richard is known for its prints, but I explained to him that my designs were solids, meant to be worn in multiple styles. We went into the showroom and Mort said, 'Put 'em on.' These were women's clothes, right? I put on the clothes, he brought in Mitsue and Carolyn Adams, the house model at the time, and before you knew it, I was Tori Richard's designer on tour on the mainland."

Prism, a vintage Tori Richard print, is freshened and reintroduced on silk crinkle chiffon for the Resort 2007 collection.

The Cotton Producers Institute featured Tori Richard in a 1970 Vogue ad.

Lisa Feldman
daughter of Janice Moody and Mort Feldman

"Before he dropped me off at college in Switzerland, we visited Paris. I remember going through the art studios. You wouldn't believe it: tiny apartments with artists in the back, floor-to-ceiling stacks of artwork, anywhere from 10x10–inch paper to 36x24 inches. This was in 1978. He would go through hundreds, maybe thousands, of sheets. He'd say, 'No. No. No. Yes. Yes. Yes.' They could be pictures, flowers, whatever; if he liked one little thing with a swish of a brush, he'd keep it. He could change the color or one little flower—a little detail.

"Even a small 16 x 10–inch sheet of paper could cost $200 or $300. I couldn't believe it. He'd end up with stacks and stacks, and I'd go, 'Dad, do you know how much this is costing?' He'd say, 'It doesn't matter, we may need it.'"

like fuschia and magenta," recalls Kotomori. "He said OK, and he was brave enough to dye the knit for me in Japan: 5,000 yards for each color, and there were at least eight or nine colors." He also used black and brown, kelly green, blue and orange, and other courageous combinations for his ethnically influenced styles.

As Tori Richard men's wear sprinted to the foreground in the 1980s and '90s, bold prints in upscale shirts captured the sizzle and commanded center stage, launching a peacock revolution in the line. In the past twelve years, under Josh Feldman's leadership, the spotlight has shifted to reflect a new balance for the new century.

Although the current collections reflect a quieter, more subdued style, accents such as beading, metallic overlays, and plush embroidery still grant the diva her stage. Silk denim is embroidered in lavish rococo patterns. Foliage-border prints in jackets and trench coats hint of safaris and desert trysts. The Arabesque print is immortal and fresh, a nod to the past and future. Carmen Miranda may be resting for now, but the drum roll still sounds.

Loungewear was popular in the 1960s, a time of dressing up for entertaining at home. Above, a cotton sateen caftan at the doors to Mort Feldman's office on Cooke Street. The carved doors were Feldman's trademark at every Tori Richard location and now form the entrance to Josh Feldman's office.

Eileen Otake
Tori Richard vice president/administration

"Mr. Feldman kept all the solicitations from charity in a shoebox. By the end of the year it was full. He never threw any away. Every year, around October or November, he and I would go through the box and separate them into mainland and local charities. Then he'd decide who would receive a check and how much. Sometimes I would tell him, 'We can't give to them; we have to help the local charities.' There were so many mainland ones. But he wanted to give to everyone! And sometimes he'd send a check in the early part of the year. And they would keep on sending letters, and I would tell him, 'We already gave.'

"Sometimes he'd hear about someone having a hard time, like a school in Wai'anae, and he would send a check on the spot. Sometimes he'd read about it in the newspaper. He cared about people. He was a very generous man."

The Tori Richard label stands for a life of enjoyment. Its casual elegance and the artistry of its prints, fabrics, and workmanship bespeak a world in which business is a means but not an end. In the world of Tori Richard, life is the beach beyond the board room, the cruise beyond the corporation, the hammock beckoning when the briefcase and laptop snap shut.

Freedom Play

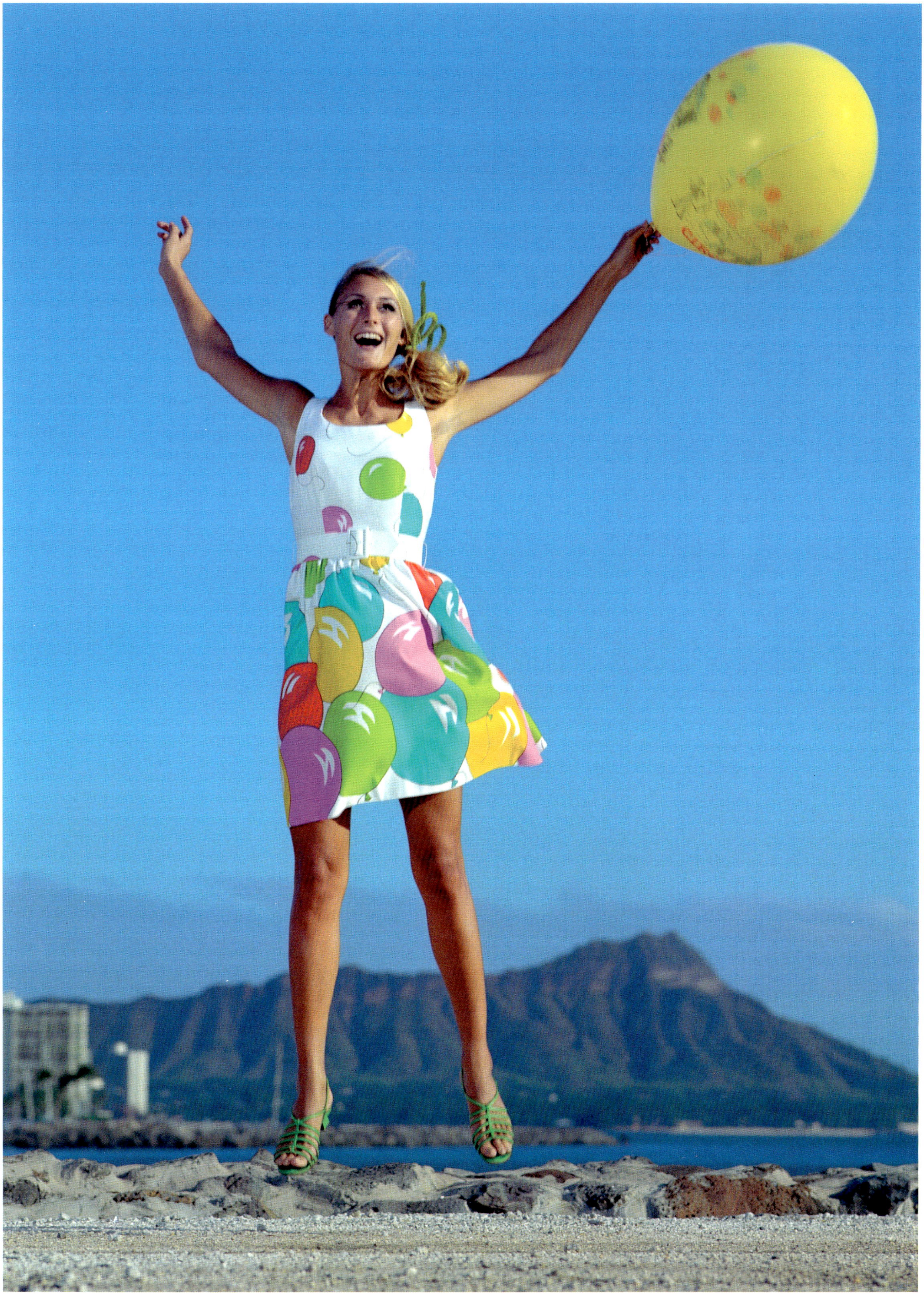

Play

Preceding page: *Diamond Head is the backdrop for this 1980 vintage Tori Richard dress, a playful headliner on Waikīkī Beach.*

Below: *From spring 2005, Paisley Paradise in cotton lawn is teamed with cotton sateen–spandex shorts in Easter colors.*

From the beginnings of the company, in the late 1950s through '60s, the swimsuit was an emblem of the leisure life. What could be more fun than the beach? The beach, pool, and patio were the ultimate symbols of relaxation, and Americans had a lot of leisure time. Today, with the world shrinking and work expanding, with communications instantaneous and compressed, moments of leisure are the uppermost currency, at the highest premium ever.

Synonymous with leisure is the resort, the hallmark of travel and escape. No matter where it is in the world, the resort is a mirror of reward—for work well done, for the long weekday commute, for work days away from the family. With their long and colorful history, Tori Richard designs reflect this world and the joys of recreation.

New collections feature dresses and separates with contemporary accents—beading, lace, a hint of Lurex—for nights on the town or intimate dinners in faraway places. Wrap skirts and camisoles, halter tops and jackets, strapless dresses and tie-front shirtdresses bear stylized images in colors of sand, ocean, and jungle-flanked waterfalls. Cargo shorts for men suggest bird-watching canopy tours in lush

Bottom left, *a vintage Tori Richard swimsuit from the 1960s.* Bottom right, *Monaco, in embroidered cotton, is paired with cotton-bamboo pants from the Fall 2005 collection.* Below, *a 1960 cotton piqué pantsuit, in front of the Aloha Tower.*

Costa Rica, or safaris in African savannas. Poolside trunks are solid or printed, in silky cotton blends and Mediterranean colors. Adventure, leisure, and practicality are imprinted in these garments, like a passport stamped on fabric.

Pareos, sarongs, drawstring pants, and tunic cover-ups come in sheer silk blends for layering over swimwear. Plush terrycloth lounge suits and robes bring comfort at home and in faraway places. Sun dresses are nostalgic and current, a Tori Richard standard, reinterpreted with fresh new touches and springtime prints in lagoon and flamingo colors. Camisoles, skirts, shorts, and long-sleeved shirts carry a fresh look forward in silk piqué knit. Poolside or beachfront, the message is playful, relaxed, and layered, with a touch of whimsy to set off the elegance.

Private contracts also speak the language of play. Harley-Davidson enthusiasts around the world are sporting Tori Richard style and quality. As the official licensee for Harley-Davidson resort apparel, Tori Richard designs its men's and women's logo wear for thousands of dealers throughout the world. Harley-Davidson shirts, swimwear, and accessories are designed and manufactured to the usual high Tori Richard standards.

Zinnia, left, in silk, and Foliage, a silk trench coat, show off engineered prints in year-round applications.

Even in the days before stretchy, quick-dry synthetics liberated the beachgoer, Tori Richard swimsuits were marvels of construction. The earliest women's suits had darts and gathers and were made of cotton. And they were hugely popular. "The cotton one- and two-piece suit had a darted, form-fitting top, and the cotton covered well," explains Tori Wickland, after whom the company is named. "This was prior to knit fabric, spandex, and nylon. Cotton didn't bind, and you were always pulling it down to cover you. No bikinis, please.

"But it held up in the surf, sand, and chlorine, and you could paddle an outrigger canoe or bodysurf in it. And it usually had a matching skirt, short, or long shirt to use as a cover-up, most welcome at the beach or pool."

Wickland's mother, Janice Feldman, established the blueprint for Tori Richard leisure wear. Even through tectonic shifts in popular tastes and lifestyles, the template has retained its luster. Her designs were a nod to Sundays and never-ending summers, to spring colors and happy prints. With their reversible swimsuits and beach cover-ups, sarong skirts, and shark-skin "patio tapers," her styles were hot to sizzling.

"Hawaiian in spirit—but without

Carnivale, in refined stretch twill from spring 2005, is meant for sun, play, and pleasure.

a single palm tree or hibiscus blossom—the real feeling is casual California at Tori Richard, Ltd., and the spring-summer line is as relaxed in silhouette and spectacular in prints as ever," raved *California Apparel News* in March 1963. "Swimsuits are one or two pieces, the latter including a bikini. One-piece suits are semi-princess-fitted or piped at the natural waistline, sometimes cuffed at the bodice top. Little boy or boxer shorts as well as skirts are shown in the swimsuit styles."[1] Accompanying the article was a "butterfly beach cover-up" featuring wide, bat-like wings and cuffed three-quarter sleeves, the epitome of beachfront drama.

High-voltage colors and dynamic images pepper the archive of play clothes and beach wear. "Go Where the Sun Is," read a Robinson's ad of 1963. "A quiet oasis of sunshine, peaceful vistas and suit-yourself activity is the goal of almost every vacationer." Others touted images like "whistle-bait suits with coordinated beach jackets for your cabana club." Fashion euphoria was rampant, centered on coastlines, sunsets, and scenery invoking "the flower-splashed happiness" of Hawai'i.

"From our made-in-Hawaii collections, we've gathered this flotilla of surf and sun clothes in

Jerry Feldman
Mort's son

"One day I saw a very fat lady wearing a Tori Richard dress, and I ran up to my dad, laughing and teasing, and said, 'Look at that fat lady…' And he looked at me really seriously and said, 'Son, every time you see one of those heavy ladies wearing a Tori Richard dress, you'd better run up to her and tell her she's beautiful, because those people put the pants on you.' It says a lot about my father's respect, not only for Tori Richard, but for people in general."

---

the limpid, underwater colors of anemones," gushed a Saks Fifth Avenue ad from the 1960s or '70s; "in petal-fresh cottons, patterned in pink or aqua—the poolsider dress." The joy of play proved timeless, propelling a part of every Tori Richard collection into the 21st century. In 2004 and 2005, *Women's Wear Daily*, *InStyle*, *OK!*, and other prominent publications featured Tori Richard leisure wear on their pages.

Hard work and creativity, strong leadership, and an enduring sense of their rewards form the engine that drives Tori Richard. Nationally and internationally, these qualities have resulted in unprecedented growth to burnish the Tori Richard star in its second generation.

"My father came back to see the company through a transition," explains Josh Feldman, who, as principal owner of the company since 1998, has spearheaded its growth. "Something like 80 percent of family businesses don't succeed to the second generation. Not only have we succeeded, but we thrived through the evolution.

"How did my father see the business after he was gone? He saw us continuing on the path that was established twelve years ago. He always asked me, 'How big do you want Tori Richard to be?' It's a matter of lifestyle. No matter how much we grow as a company, we never want to lose the fun."

Preceding page: From the Fall 2006 collection comes Tie-Dye Palm, beaded on cotton voile, comfortable enough for lounging. Top, Orchid Road in silk crepe de chine is a Resort 2006 design. Far right: a vintage jumpsuit; near right, Hot House on silk interlock, from the Resort 2007 collection, is no garden-variety wrap dress.

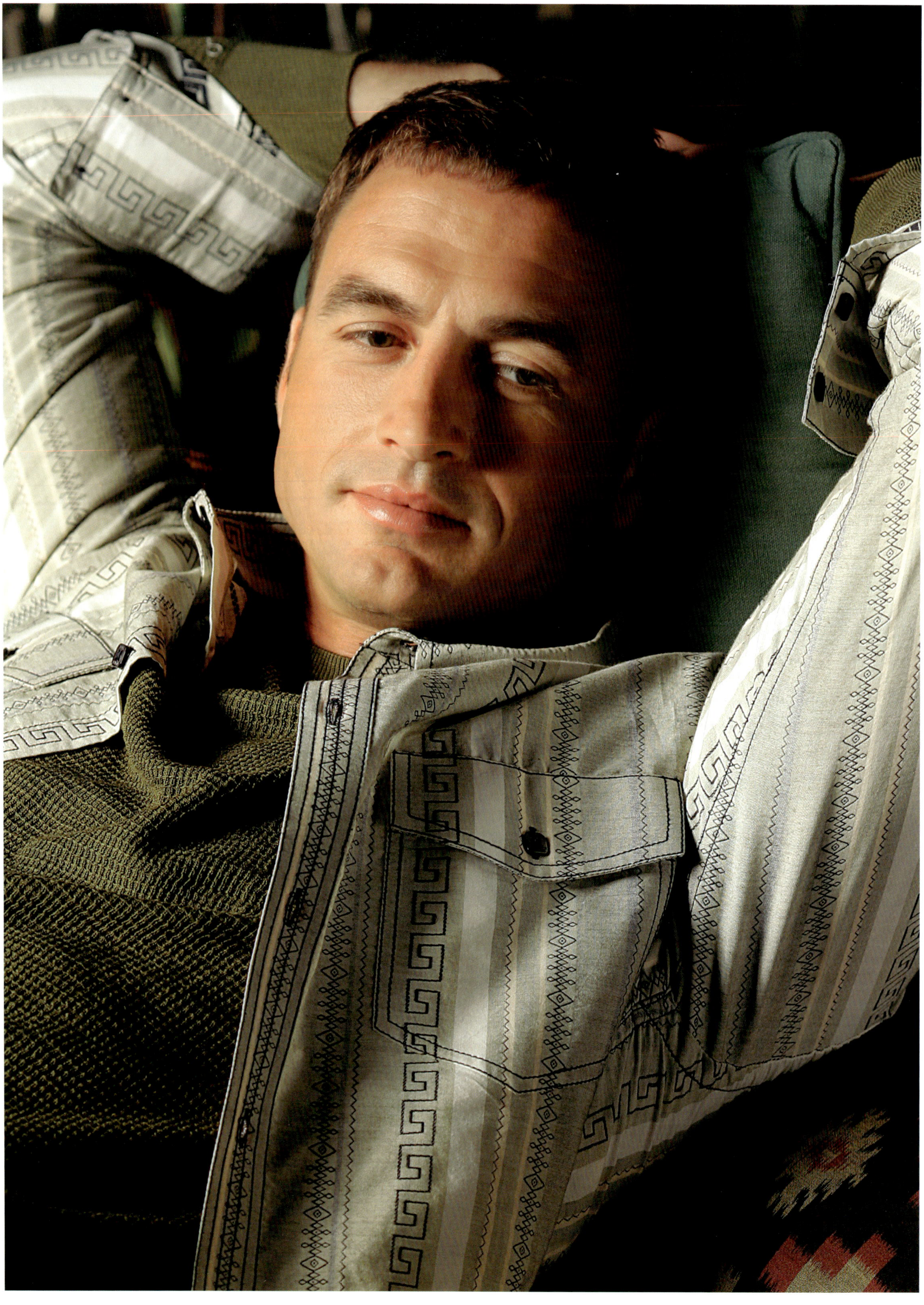

Josh Feldman points to the Tori Richard prints that appear vibrantly on his oversized computer screen. The prints have names like Midnight, Orient Express, Trumpetini, Fossil, Mediterranean, Mandarin, Murano – tens of thousands of them in the database, names that circle the globe, that conjure up five-star resorts in exotic destinations and lifestyles of leisure and confidence. Their fabrics are top-quality silks, very fine cottons, and blends, and their images are evocative and eclectic, as if telling stories of ocean crossings and far-flung ports – or even just a backyard pool party – where taste and romance run high.

Man of the House

Man of the House

Preceding page: *Bohemian Stripe, in cotton yarn-dyed jacquard.* Top: *embroidered front panel in cotton,* and above, *cotton shirts from 1972.*

"We may be located in Honolulu, but we are not a Hawaiian shirt company," Feldman declares, pointing to the stylized designs and the unique, occasionally semi-abstract Asian and Mediterranean motifs. "I won't make any bones about it, but we *were* an aloha shirt company during my father's absence." Feldman speaks forcefully about how the company had fallen into a morass of dated products, an economic downturn, and the limitations of a stereotype—an aloha shirt company—that combined to imperil Tori Richard. Not only had the company "deteriorated" into such a state, he adds, but Tori Richard's market had shriveled to mostly Hawai'i, its once robust mainland sales a shadow of their former days. Mainland showrooms were closed, and the company had all but totally withdrawn from the women's business.

"During the period the family was out of the business, the company made primarily men's shirts," Feldman continues. "It was a resort wear company that made dramatic prints. It was always the print, the art of the print, which formed the core of the company. Somehow we had gotten away from that during my father's absence. Returning to our roots, returning to the print, was the emphasis of our revitalization."

Josh Feldman's good-natured zeal and sense of purpose are well known among industry observers, who have watched Tori Richard, under his direction, reclaim its prominence with a vengeance. Part of Feldman's conviction comes from the knowledge that Tori Richard, originally a stylish women's fashion house, has always distinguished itself from the kitsch associated with the Hawaiian shirt.

Juline Fujii, men's sportswear buyer for Nordstrom stores from 1997 to 2005, says she watched "Josh grow into being in charge. It was fun watching him evolve into that leadership role. And I could see the line evolve with him. He has helped to update the line and keep it current while not diverging from the root of Tori Richard, and without letting go of its history."

The changes, she observes, include fresh ideas in Tori Richard's print art. "Instead of being Hawaiian floral, they started to move into geometrics, which blended nicely. They're offering something different to someone who doesn't want a Hawaiian flower shirt."

But for someone who does want a floral shirt, she adds, "As far as quality goes, Tori Richard raised the bar in the Hawaiian shirt

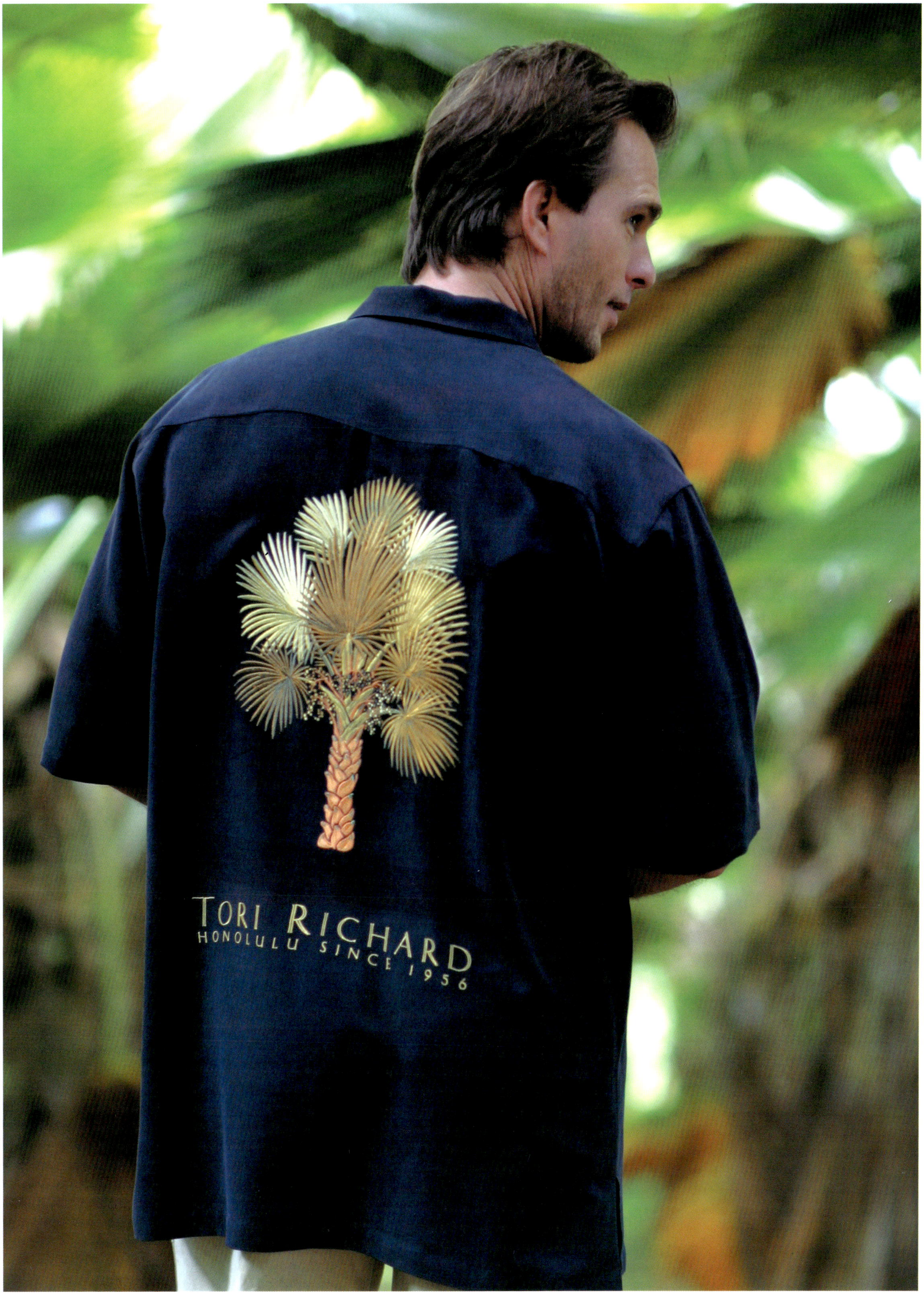
TORI RICHARD
HONOLULU SINCE 1956

Natural fibers are the Tori Richard staple, as in the silk embroidered Palm Tree, preceding page; Shutter Weave, below, and cotton, yarn-dyed jacquard men's shirts, bottom.

industry. The Tori Richard quality level was what everyone had to step up and match."

The defining factor is the product, not the location, explains Jim Fisher, the company's New York men's showroom representative. "It's easy to perceive a company in Hawai'i that makes shirts as a Hawaiian shirt line, but when buyers examine the product, they know they're looking at something different—an entire resort line of top quality," he says.

"When Josh interviewed me in New York ten years ago, I asked him whether this was a shirt shop or a print shop. He did not miss a beat. He immediately said, 'We are a print house.'"

Upstairs from Feldman's office, Tori Richard collections are designed, shown, stored, and shipped to thousands of retail stores around the globe that cater to a broad audience of worldly, quality-conscious wearers. Among those stores are Nordstrom and the hugely successful Garys & Co. shops of Fashion Island, Newport Beach.

"A lot of men who buy the Tori Richard shirts don't need new shirts," observes Dick Braeger, owner of Garys & Co. shops. "They collect them, they keep them. That's why Tori Richard stands out—it's a collection. We get the

Revel, a paisley print in cotton knit, is from the Resort 2006 collection. Bottom, Panelrama, from 2005, is in silk twill with a windowpane effect.

most avid collectors coming in. Think about it: How many plumeria shirts do you need?

"Most of the other lines look pretty much the same, but these are unique, and always for a higher-end, more sophisticated buyer," he adds. "You can wear Tori Richard as nice sportswear, with a jacket. This is contemporary resort wear rather than Hawaiian wear." Tropical chic is not excluded, but the key word is "chic," not "kitsch," say observers.

Who is the Tori Richard man? He is, says Fujii, "someone who works hard during the week, likes to go on vacation, spends time with the family, and goes out to nice dinners." He is a year-round leisure lover who moves easily among different worlds; a baby boomer or his son, perhaps, in search of versatile resort wear for his life and travels. He peruses the print, the colors, and the "hand"—industry parlance for the feel of the fabric—as well as the weights of the silks and fine cottons, gauging their appropriateness for the climate and ambience of his next destination. The shirts are coordinated with bottoms in different fabrications and styles, from trousers to shorts to swimwear.

Fabrications—butter-soft goat suede, silk twill, Peruvian Pima cotton, silk-cotton jacquards, cotton dobby jacquards, spun viscose, cotton-nylon, Tencel®, and the company's proprietary cotton lawn finish—are rich and wide-ranging. Custom-made, authentic shell buttons, favored over coconut buttons for their superior quality, discreetly bear the Tori Richard name, and flat French seams are a smooth and tidy finish. The attention to detail is unflagging, and the influences—Asian, Mediterranean, Caribbean, tropical, or urban-chic—suggest spirited travel and adventure.

From its beginnings, when it was busy designing women's wear, the company has marched to its own drum and dominated its own separate universe. Not so much contrarian as independent, riding its success in classically sophisticated women's fashion, Tori Richard made women's clothing almost exclusively until 1969—thirteen years after its 1956 opening. The late '60s was a period of parallel universes: Hawaiian shirts were increasingly kitsch, slick disco was king, and natural fibers hibernated in the shadow of synthetics. When Tori Richard introduced its men's shirts in 1969, it was at the request of retailer Liberty House. Using for its men's shirts the head-turning prints from its women's line, Tori Richard was catapulted into the men's resort apparel business and

For the year-round Tori Richard man: an embroidered cotton sweater, below, and Circle Line, in lightweight cotton lawn.

has never looked back.

Out of the starting block shot the "polyester suede" men's shirts in the '70s, followed by the reverse-print cotton Cooke Street line in 1980. "The men's line was always based on the Tori Richard print selection, not styles which consisted of a short-sleeve cotton shirt with basic and button-down collar and reverse printing," notes Jesse Goodman, vice president of the men's division from 1977 to 1988. "It was about the appreciation of quality as the prime ingredient of the product."

In men's wear, as with women's wear, the company combined its affinity for print and art with the finest in available fabrics and workmanship. The classic late bloomer, Tori Richard men's wear sprinted ahead in a crowded field and now accounts for a lion's share of the company's business.

In a *Pacific Business News* article on June 25, 2004, Tori Richard's niche was described as "the upscale, well-traveled customer who can afford to pay $100 for a silk aloha shirt." The article reported that the opening of Tori Richard retail stores in resort and hotel-resort areas was a response to consumer demand and opportunities in a hot retail market.[1] Today that turf is greener, more fertile, and better manicured than it's ever been: Some 2,500 upscale shops across the U.S., Asia, Europe, and the Caribbean sell the Tori Richard line.

The collection includes an updated resort component, with narrower silhouettes and modernized prints. The shirts are in the finest fabrics of the day, from silk jacquards with custom-designed woven motifs to supple Tencel® and sun-loving Egyptian cotton lawn. There are bold embroidered motifs, and even no motifs at all on the solid knit jerseys. There are crew-neck knits and easy sweaters, polo-style shirts and still some tropicals, as well as men's trousers of corded Tencel® and poolside trunks of sanded cotton and nylon.

"With this line, you can't say it's just one style of printing or design," reflects Lauren Yep. "Retrospectively, Tori Richard has had various print trends. They've always done well with tropicals, and they have their Asian periods."

Josh Feldman discontinued the polyester shirts in the early 1990s, when they were replaced with embroidery, jacquards, and various treatments and fabric innovations.

Matched pockets are a given, and matched fronts a must in the engineered prints, a standout in the men's line since the 1990s, when Feldman joined the company and reintroduced the concept. The

*Dramatic prints in polyester suede were popular in the
1970s and '80s. Lower right: From 2004, the
embroidered dragon on silk continues over the shoulder
and down the back.*

All hands on deck: three men in a rowboat, 1981.

Bottom, a dressier Tori Richard man, in silk.

prints had a highly successful, nearly decade-long run before they were discontinued in 2001.

"Josh brought back some of the old engineered looks in rayon for men," recalls Mark Troedson, the company's Pacific sales director. "The women's line was the big thing when I started, and it was always engineered gowns in beautiful prints, such as border prints on the bottom. They were all unique."

Patio was a top-selling men's engineered print, a technical marvel: cocktails on a tray and asymmetric foliage on the sleeves, body, and collar, all elements and design matched to a T. Patio's signature was the complex print engineering: the tray tilted just so, the lemon wedge bridging the flawlessly matched front, every leaf of the foliage perfectly matched on sleeves, front, collar, and pocket. In homage to Nik-Nik, an erstwhile clothing company that put a number to every print, each of the engineered prints was sequentially numbered.

Those prints reflected the leisure-loving spirit of the times, a time in which fabrics, in impressive new weaves and textures, perfectly accommodated the prevailing lifestyle. In her book, *The End of Fashion*, Teri Agins points out that nationally, casual apparel was on a definite roll.

"Throughout the 1990s, sport shirts and khakis had displaced suits to become the de rigueur office uniform, even at the most traditional Wall Street firms like Goldman Sachs and JP Morgan, which finally succumbed to the 'all casual all the time' edict in 2000 in order to better fit in with a new generation of young Internet entrepreneurs who were rewriting America's business culture," she writes. "The pervasive casual trend had succeeded in stunning Saks Fifth Avenue, which conceded that it was having a harder time selling its stockpile of dressy designer creations."[2]

Tori Richard fell into step with the zeitgeist and reinvented itself on several levels. When mainland manufacturers began copying the prints, Tori Richard retained its edge in the form of embroidery. It embellished top-quality silk fabrics with dramatically embroidered and engineered designs of large fan palms, lion fish, martinis, and other emblems of whimsy and beauty. Select pieces feature hidden, sometimes risqué, embroidery inside the pockets, as well as other unique touches. These shirts are instantly recognizable as top-of-the-line Tori Richard signature pieces.

"In designs like Chill Out, we had the enlarged martini on the

Left: *Eames*, in silk/linen from Resort 2006, carries the timeless geometric theme. *Graphic Flower*, bottom, and *Dragon Back*, below, are leisurewear winners from Summer 2004.

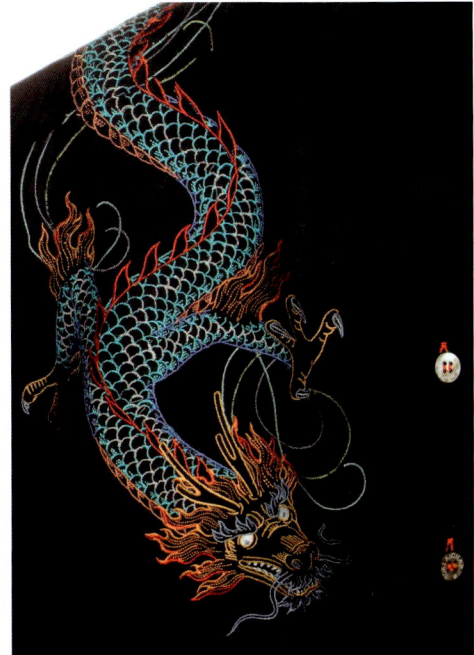

Resort 2005 presents Capri Solid in silk, a beach-to-evening look for the sun-loving man.

back of the shirt, and maybe just a little martini glass on the front, or something inside the pocket that was unique," explained Mark Troedson.

Many weights and textures of silk replaced rayon, and the fabrics became finer as the textile industry developed new fibers, weaves and textures. "We've evolved light years from those early days in terms of fabrication, sophistication of prints, and the completeness of offerings," comments Jim Fisher. "We're also addressing a younger-thinking guy of today than we ever have, and we are perceived as a very fine collection, not just a shirt line."

While the engineered silks are notable for their designs and lavish craftsmanship, it's prints like Murano and Marquesas, in Egyptian cotton lawn, that remain Tori Richard staples. "These are the shirts we ship over and over again, of the same print and the same color," said Troedson. They are quiet, reliable shirts—the antithesis of the stereotypical Hawaiian shirt, a genre with its own humor and its own passionate following.

"Hawaiian shirts are a mood-altering substance," writes novelist Mark Lindquist, in a state of tropical-shirt euphoria. "Wearing one gives a man license to laugh too loud, drink too much, leapfrog parking meters, be savage, and run amok.

"This shirt has a voice. It shouts." Lindquist, who bought his first Hawaiian shirt in a thrift shop in the late 1970s, delivers a delightful, punchy soliloquy on the subject in the August 1991 issue of *Details* magazine. An attorney by day in Tacoma, Washington, he writes of the rite of passage that the shirt represented to him. It elicited "brash," "zany" behavior, he said. As if discussing a sartorial loss of virginity or an existential bar mitzvah, he writes, "No matter how you wear yours, prepare to be transformed."[3]

Instead of transforming themselves, Josh and Mort Feldman transformed their company. In the senior Feldman's lifetime, he went from manufacturing children's coats out of surplus wool blankets to selling its polar opposite: expensively made, labor-intensive prints that have made their mark in an upscale market.

"Mort just loved creating things," said Jim Romig, chairman and founder of Hilo Hattie. "If he bought an apartment, he'd tear out the walls and do it right. Cost was not an issue when he wanted to do something. It just had to be done right, and it was the same with the clothing he made."

Dale Hope
author of *The Aloha Shirt: Spirit of the Islands*

"Tori Richard brought a lot of sophistication to Island garment manufacturing—styling, silhouette, a flair for print. Mort Feldman was one of the most competitive manufacturers, certainly in Hawai'i, and he was able to fit in with the larger women's fashion houses from New York to California. He was able to incorporate his sensitivity to Asian art and design into his lines of women's wear. The Orient and its sophistication gave Mort endless inspiration for his art and designs, and he always made sure that he had designers working by his side to effectively implement his vision. He was a pioneer who brought bold newness to the local and mainland marketplace."

Tori Richard men's wear comes in a plethora of fabrics, such as spun viscose, below, and tangerine silk jacquard, bottom, in a subtle banana leaf design.

Tori Richard's men's shirts range from traditional Hawaiian and tribal motifs to Asian and nature-based prints. Although Tori Richard did not make men's apparel in quantity until the late 1960s, some of these shirts are likely to have been made in the late 1950s. Vintage Tori Richard shirts, primarily in cotton and polyester, still circulate on the Internet and are coveted by shirt collectors.

Tori Richard shirts reflect
craftsmanship, style, and a lifestyle
of leisure and enjoyment. A
pacesetter in the technology of the
engineered print, Tori Richard has
an archive of prints that numbers
in the tens of thousands, growing
by the hundreds every month.
Among the notable details: French
seams, collar stands, and matched
pockets. Tori Richard pioneered the
reintroduction of matched fronts in
men's shirts.

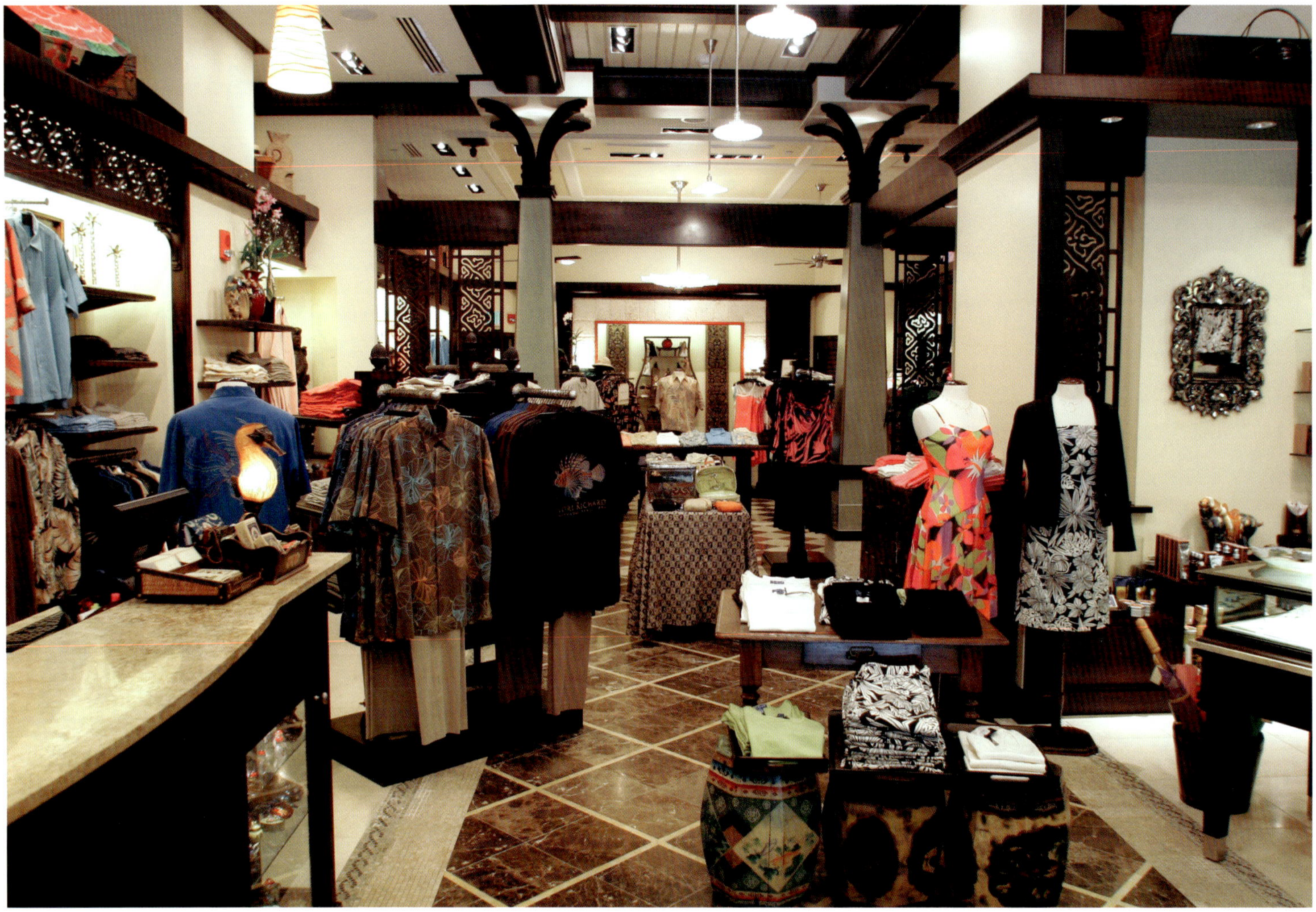

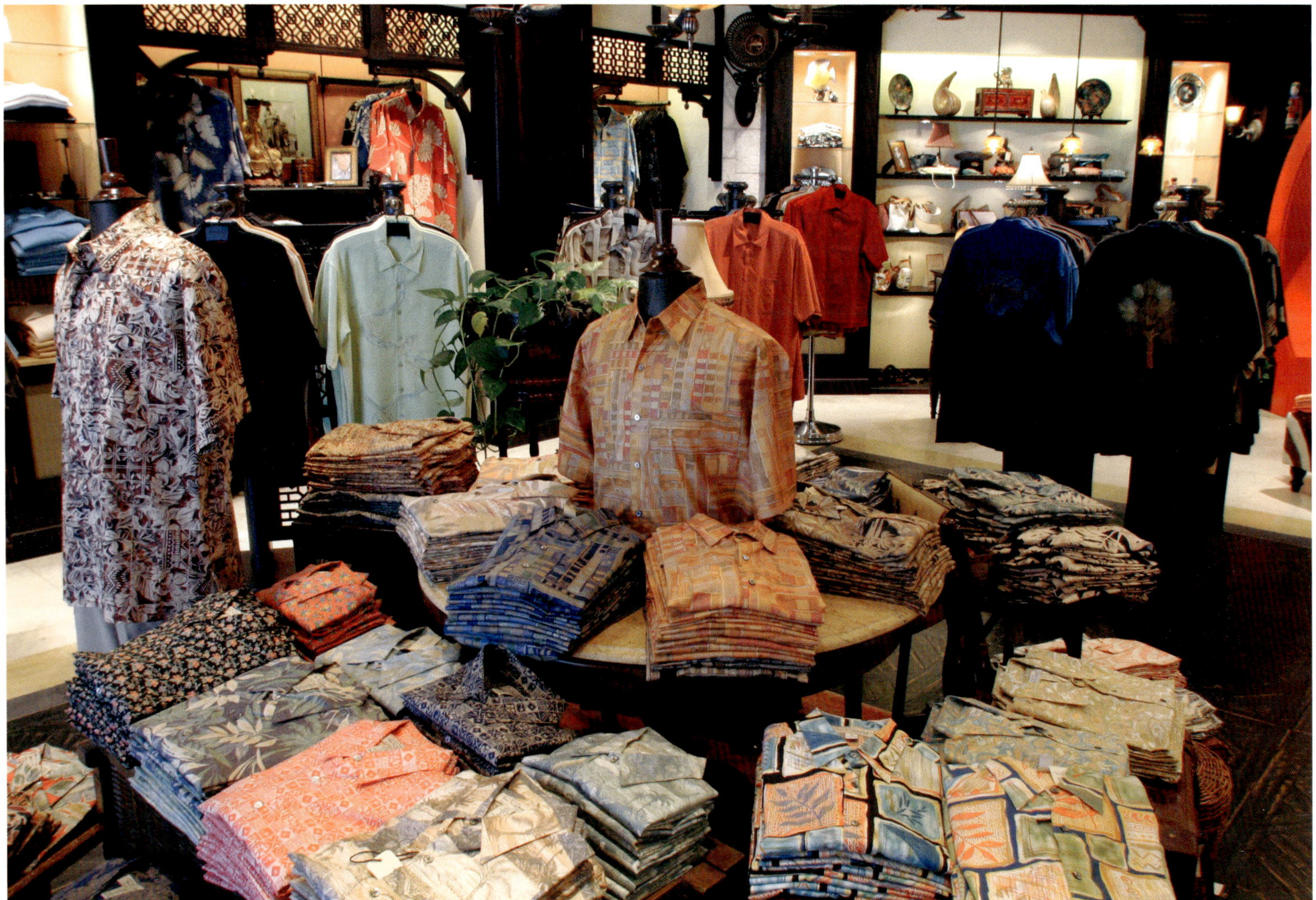

From his launching pad in Honolulu, Tori Richard CEO Josh Feldman crisscrosses the globe frequently, in perpetual motion, flying east and west with ease, bridging the worlds that form the matrix of his company. Tori Richard is ideally situated for Feldman's regular trips to France, New York, and Asia. These destinations figure prominently in Tori Richard's culture, its business growth and aesthetic vision: textile, art, and trade shows in Paris and New York, printers in Japan and China, and silk mills and manufacturing in China. In Hawai'i, where these influences coalesce as the Tori Richard brand, Feldman and his covey of designers, artists, merchandisers, and sales people integrate these elements as they pore over the collections and delivery schedules that determine the future of the company.

Encore

Encore

Josh Feldman opens the Ala Moana Center store for its blessing in November 2004.

The company is growing at a phenomenal pace, and Feldman is only 34 years old. Fresh out of college in 1994, he came aboard at his father's urging and faced a daunting task: to repair a business suffering from his father's more than decade-long absence, and to reclaim the glory of its earlier days. Accomplishing those goals called for a combination of moxie, creativity, and common sense: downsizing and outsourcing, as minimally as possible; fashions slimmed down and edgier, updated to include a younger, hipper clientele; and a refining and redefining of the brand as an upper-end resort wear manufacturer for women *and* men—not just nationally, but internationally.

Industry observers and employees say there is no doubt that Josh Feldman saved Tori Richard when it was most vulnerable. "At one point, until Mort came back to the company with Josh, Tori Richard was manufacturing mostly men's wear for the Hawai'i market," explains Ralph Odenberg, Tori Richard's West Coast men's sales representative. "The first thing they did was upgrade the image and clean up the men's wear line. Then Josh turned his attention to women's wear. He's definitely headed upstream, to higher-end goods. At this stage, it's all about his vision." This, observers agree, is where the company got its new start, and almost certainly where its future lies.

The profile and future are exceedingly rosy, with units sold and revenue figures outpacing anything the company has achieved before. Josh Feldman also initiated the recent openings of four retail Tori Richard lifestyle stores throughout Hawai'i, and there are plans for more, in the Islands and beyond. In the freestanding Tori Richard stores, clothing, accessories, and collectibles for the home reflect a cohesive, exotic East-West aesthetic and a clearly defined demographic: a sophisticated, worldly, well-read traveler of discerning tastes and with disposable income. In distancing itself from the tropical-wear genre in which it excelled, but refused to be locked into, Tori Richard has successfully retooled and moved uptown. Feldman acknowledges that there will always be tropically influenced products, but also, more importantly, resort-appropriate products. Under the younger Feldman, the growth rate has exceeded 600 percent in the past several years, with new and burgeoning markets in the finest resort centers of the world.

"This is our new showroom," says

In Honolulu, the Tori Richard stores in Ala Moana Center and the Hyatt Regency, Kalākaua Avenue, display their men's and women's wear with lifestyle accessories in an East-West ambience.

Bottom: *Josh and Mort Feldman in 1998, and below, the interior of the Wailea, Maui store.*

Josh Feldman, waving his hand over the impeccably lit, nearly completed hub of his Honolulu headquarters. "We've been here 15 years; it was time to renovate and freshen up."

The showroom is symbolic of the new face of Tori Richard. Tropical designs will be a part of the collection as long as customers demand them, but these days, they are considered yesterday, and it's the looks of tomorrow that dominate the showroom. Coordinated collections of knits and solids, cotton weaves and jacquards, denims and silks, and state-of-the-art, long-sleeved, slimmer-cut men's shirts and trousers are unveiled here. The women's fashions are simple or tailored but always contemporary, edgier and more European than ever, constructed in couture standards of quality, but without the couture price points. Fabric prints roam the world, from Asia and the Pacific to the Mediterranean, Europe, and across the U.S. The prints and styles—from cardigans to diaphanous dresses to urban-chic denim coordinates—fit easily into the glamorous scenarios of Monaco, Rio, St. Tropez, Bali, Las Vegas, Paris, and other exotic destinations of the world.

"As a resort apparel firm, our artwork is a fusion of the elements of the resort lifestyle," explains

Feldman. "We will always be primarily print-driven, so the art of the print will change with the times, just as it has for the past fifty years." What will not change, he says, is Tori Richard's core identity as a company wedded to the highest standards of quality.

"We are print-driven and identified with beautiful prints, but first and foremost, we do beautiful, sophisticated resort design," says Odenberg. "We've always kept a balance in offering prints that are sophisticated and artsy. People can look at certain prints and say, 'That's a Tori Richard.' That means we've gone way beyond the tropical genre."

An heir to his father's business radar and visionary instincts, Feldman sees Tori Richard's long-term growth as a generational transition. Inheriting a family business, he says, presented its own unique challenges. "I didn't walk into a turnkey operation, and I wasn't handed a silver spoon," he explains. "We were in great difficulty and on the verge of bankruptcy when I showed up. Our challenge has been to keep the product relevant. As the generation that we've been catering to moves on, we have to be sure that we have the right product and brand image that appeals to the one succeeding it."

In a nod to Asian tradition, temple lions guard the entrance to the Kalākaua Avenue store. Bottom: women's apparel and accessories in the Ala Moana Center store.

Below: Southeast Asian accents at Tori Richard, the Shops at Wailea, Maui. Bottom, from left: Richard, Josh, and Jerry Feldman at the opening of the Ala Moana Center store in November 2004.

While staying ahead of the needs of his customers, Feldman also looks inward, to the internal workings of a family business. "While Tori Richard, Ltd. has…opened four retail stores in Hawai'i, the vast majority of our business comes from outside the state," he wrote in an article for *MidWeek* in December of 2004.[1] "This means that many of our employees need to travel, work in sync with mainland working hours, and be able to accommodate constantly changing situations. Family businesses tend to be much more nimble and responsive to change.

"The National Federation of Independent Business claims somewhere between 75 percent and 95 percent of businesses in this country are 'small family businesses.' By most standards, Tori Richard, Ltd. is not a small business. We have well over 100 employees… However, after nearly a half-century of business in Hawai'i, we still think and act like a small family business. This is part of our longevity in the notoriously unstable apparel industry."

Feldman notes with pride the company's demographics: a mother and daughter, two husband-and-wife couples, and, until his father died in 2004, a father and son, all working in the same company. The Feldmans have considered it smart business to support such a corporate

The Wailea shop, below, features eclectic wares for the worldly. Bottom, from left: Jim Macdonald, Staci-Li Nohara, Mary-Jo Odenberg, Josh Feldman, Sue Sanders, Lee Cheatham, Sherrie Macdonald, and Mark Troedson represent a part of the Tori Richard family. Standing is Ralph Odenberg.

culture, and the proof is in the numbers: some employees have worked there for twenty, thirty, and forty years.

"*Entrepreneur* magazine and many other sources note that only thirty percent of family businesses survive the transition to the second generation," Feldman continued. "We…are fortunate not only to be in that thirty percent, but to have thrived and grown during the many years of transition.

"Being a family business has given us the strength and resiliency to persevere. If you work in a family business…you may know about the many advantages of working in a company where the management cares about what happens, not only because it's their job, but because it is their family."

acknowledgments

Although writing a book is hard work, there are several things that make it pleasurable: the collaboration and support of others, the excitement of seeing the first modest thoughts bubbling out of the blank screen, and the rekindling of recollections that invariably results from such an endeavor. The knowledge and enthusiasm of generous collaborators give shape to the vague stirrings of intention and add a lot more fun to the job.

Because I never had the pleasure of meeting Mort Feldman, I relied on the stories and reminiscences of others, and on Tori Richard's extensive and well-kept archives. All those involved in the preparation of this book lead hectic daily lives that I interrupted with great urgency and regularity, and I was met, always, with gracious cooperation.

I owe a debt of gratitude to the following people: Ellie Yamada, Eileen Otake, Amy Renshaw, Bobbie Taum, Amos Kotomori, Al Sieverts, Carolyn Adams, Penny Cardoza, Stan Morketter, Leonard Poliandro, Kim Scoggins, Jim Romig, Dale Hope, Lauren Yep, Ralph Odenberg, Jim Fisher, Mark Troedson, Karen and Don MacRae, Doreen Kapuakela, Agatha Karpowicz, Mitsue Aka, Chiyoko Ige, June Feldman, Lisa Feldman, Jerry Feldman, Diana Snyder, Nat Norfleet, and all those who were interviewed and consulted for this book. Special thanks go to Sue Sanders, whose idea for a fiftieth anniversary commemorative volume is finally realized, and to Tori Wickland, who provided valuable insights and material about her mother, Janice Moody.

If there is a keeper of visual records of Tori Richard, it's Jerry Chong, who spent decades photographing Tori Richard designs. When we needed to capture the Tori Richard of today, it was Jerry Chong, along with photographer Richard Feldman, Mort Feldman's son, who created the images with admirable ease and skill.

We made every effort to locate and secure permission from the photographers, publishers, advertising agencies, and writers for all of the archival material, some of which is over forty years old. Some of the publications have long been out of print. If I have failed to credit anyone properly, it is not for lack of trying, and I offer my heartfelt apologies.

Donna Burns, former Tori Richard designer, brought her gifts and tenacity to the job as project coordinator. With Uʻilani Mokiao, her partner in Facelift, their design company, Donna was invaluable in the day-to-day demands of coordination, communication, and styling.

I also thank three women whose contributions to my professional life and peace of mind are beyond measure: the ever-reliable and competent Sandra Acuña, who spared no inconvenience in preparing the Endnotes, References, and Index; Dawn Sueoka, a tireless and eagle-eyed proofreader; and Joyce Libby, my long-time friend and copy-editor.

Designer Bud Linschoten's character and artistry are imprinted on every page of this book. He was always present with a kind and encouraging word for others, even as he confronted his own monumental tasks and sifted through thousands of images and last-minute changes to bring form and sparkle to the book.

Our maestro, Josh Feldman, led the entire effort. I met him a few months after Mort died, when personal loss—the loss of a father—was fresh and raw and the burden of expectation no doubt weighed heavily upon him. Having assumed the company's responsibilities in 2001 and its presidency in 2004, Josh was a natural leader who had long been groomed to ensure a stable and reassuring continuity for the company, as well as prominent growth. Tori Richard has flourished under his stewardship, and it is through nothing other than his own smarts and commitment and a work ethic that flies in the face of often misguided notions of succession. Josh has revealed natural editorial skills; he was a pleasure to work with and remained unflappable under deadline pressures and the rigors of travel and business.

I hope this book succeeds in chronicling not only Tori Richard's fashion story, but also the challenges and triumphs of a family business as it enters a new generation with heart and soul intact.

To the Feldmans, the Tori Richard staff, and the inaugural team of this, our first project for Hula Moon Press, *mazel tov* and mahalo.

Jocelyn Fujii

references

Agins, Teri. *The End of Fashion: How Marketing Changed the Clothing Business Forever.* New York, NY: Harper Collins Publishers, 1999.

Arthur, Linda B. *Aloha Attire: Hawaiian Dress in the Twentieth Century.* Atglen, PA: Schiffer Publishing, Ltd., 1999.

Beacon (Honolulu, HI), "Hawaii's Glamour Garments," April 1962, 8.

Bergdorf Goodman. Advertisement. 1969 (Tori Richard archive).

California Apparel News (Los Angeles, CA), September 30, 1977.

California Apparel News (Los Angeles, CA), "Semi-fit Lines, Torrid Prints at Tori Richard," March 1, 1963.

Dallas Times Herald (Dallas, TX), "Hawaii Heads into Dallas," April 20, 1969.

Donnelly, Dave. "Dave Donnelly's Hawaii," *Honolulu Star-Bulletin,* September 23, 1980.

Evans, Cleo. "Fashions Spur 'Ice Capades,'" *Sunday Star-Bulletin & Advertiser* (Honolulu, HI), February 17, 1963.

Feldman, Josh, "Mixing Family with Business, Business Round Table," *MidWeek* (Kaneohe, HI), December 15, 2004.

Hawaii Dept. of Business, Economic Development & Tourism. *Hawaii Gross State Product Accounts, 1958–1985; Summary Estimates 1986, 1987, and 1988.* Honolulu, HI, 1989.

HongKong Standard (Hong Kong), "Summer-Autumn Wear Show," July 28, 1973.

Hope, Dale, and Gregory Tozian. *The Aloha Shirt: Spirit of the Islands.* Hillsboro, OR: Beyond Words Publishing, 2000.

Lindquist, Mark, "Hawaiian Punch," *Details* (New York, NY), August 1991.

Natarajan, Prabha, "Tori Richard Ready to Outfox Tommy," *Pacific Business News* (Charlotte, NC), June 25, 2004.

Ricardo, Diana, "For Women—Not Teeners or Tweeners," *Vancouver Sun* (Vancouver, BC), March 25, 1966.

Saks Fifth Avenue. Advertisement. (Tori Richard archive).

Taylor, Lois, "Fire Sale Gets More Than it Bargained For," *Honolulu Star-Bulletin* (Honolulu, HI), June 2, 1973.

notes

The Endless Summer
1. Arthur, *Aloha Attire,* 66.
2. *Beacon,* "Hawaii's Glamour Garments."
3. Hawaii Dept. of Business, Economic Development & Tourism. *Hawaii Gross State Product Accounts, 1958–1985,* 17.
4. *California Apparel News,* Sept. 30, 1977.
5. Taylor, "Fire Sale Gets More Than It Bargained For."

The Art of the Print
1. Hope, *The Aloha Shirt,* 84.

Tori Glory
1. Ricardo, "For Women—Not Teeners or Tweeners."
2. Bergdorf Goodman. Advertisement.
3. Saks Fifth Avenue. Advertisement.

Torigami
1. Donnelly, "Dave Donnelly's Hawaii."

Grand Entrance
1. Evans, "Fashions Spur 'Ice Capades.'"
2. *Dallas Times Herald,* "Hawaii Heads into Dallas."

3. Ibid.
4. Ibid.
5. Agins, *The End of Fashion,* 87.
6. Ibid.
7. *HongKong Standard,* "Summer-Autumn Wear Show."

Play
1. *California Apparel News,* "Semi-fit Lines, Torrid Prints at Tori Richard," 1.

Man of the House
1. Natarajan, "Tori Richard Ready to Outfox Tommy."
2. Agins, *The End of Fashion,* 276.
3. Lindquist, "Hawaiian Punch," 36.

Encore
1. Feldman, "Mixing Family with Business, Business Round Table," 36.

Photo Credits
Whitney Anderson: 81
Tom Brown: 80
Jerry Chong: 12 bottom, 15, 17, 21, 24, 25, 28, 29, 32, 35, 36 right, 37, 38, 39 top left and bottom, 40 top, 41 left, 42 top and bottom, 43, 45, 46 top right, 47 top and bottom, 49, 50, 54, 55 top, 57 top, 59, 61 top, 68 bottom, 70 bottom, 71 top, 73 left and top, 74, 78 top, 85, 87 top, 94 bottom, 99, 100 top, 104, 105
Josh Feldman: 56 top left; second, third and bottom right
Richard Feldman: 11, 13, 14, 16, 33, 42 middle, 46 left, 52 bottom right, 53 bottom left, 55 bottom left, 56 bottom, 61 bottom, 64, 65, 67, 70 top, 72 top and bottom right, 76-77, 78 bottom, 82 right, 83 right, 87 bottom left, 88 right, 106, 108-109, 110 top, 111
Jon Mozo: 68 top
Mike Seiji: 82 top right, 88
Brett Uprichard: 110 bottom
Ian White: 91 bottom left
Courtesy of *Tori Wickland:* 19, 20 lower right, 22 (telegram), 31 (*Vogue* reprint)
Page 3: Esther Wolf ad in *Houston Post,* April 5, 1970
Page 8-9: Fall Holiday Tori Richard line, photographed at La Pietra, 1976

index

A
African influence, 76
Aka, Mitsue, 11, 20, 26, 52, 53, 57
Aloha Friday, 29
Aloha Kai, 40
Arnel®, 61, 76
Asian influence, 30, 47, 66, 68–69.
  see also Japanese influence

B
Ball, Lucille, 20
Bergdorf Goodman, 11, 26, 61
Best & Co., 11
Bloomingdale's, 73, 79
Braeger, Dick, 96
Burns, Donna, 47, 55
buttons, 55, 97

C
California Apparel News, 28, 89
Cardin, Pierre, 80
cartel, 18, 29, 40, 70
Chamberlain, Richard, 72
Chong, Jerry, 54
cloth. *see* fabrics
collar, 51, 56
collection, 64, 77, 80, 81, 82, 90, 97
company evolution, 22, 29, 32, 82, 97
company headquarters
  Pier 7 factory (Honolulu Harbor), 20
  Primo Brewery factory (Cooke St.), 20, 30
  Quonset hut factory (Beretania St.), 20
convertible dresses line, 80
Cooke Street line, 32, 98
coordinated fashions, 64, 79, 97, 110
Cosco, Bob, 30
cotton, 25, 56, 61, 62, 70, 76, 88
cotton lawn, 31, 43, 44, 47, 56, 63, 98, 102
cotton sateen, 25
cotton surah, 61

D
Dacron®, 61, 76
Dallas Times Herald, 78
Darnel®, 76
denim, 64, 78, 82, 110
design protection, 43
designs, 43, 44, 47, 62, 68, 70, 75, 82, 86, 87, 89, 100
Details magazine, 103
Dior, Christian, 80
dobbies, 25

E
engineered prints, 23, 33, 53, 62, 63, 64, 98, 100. *see also* prints
Evans, Cleo, 78

F
fabrics
  Arnel®, 61, 76
  cotton, 25, 56, 61, 70, 72, 76, 88
  cotton lawn, 27, 43, 44, 47, 56, 63, 98, 102
  cotton sateen, 25
  cotton surah, 61
  Dacron®, 61, 76
  Darnel®, 76
  denim, 64, 78, 82, 110
  dobbies, 25
  greige goods, 34
  jacquard, 47, 97, 98, 110
  jersey, 64, 98
  Maharani silk, 61. *see also* silk piqué, 25
  Polyplush, 61, 80
  rayon, 56, 72, 100, 102
  sharkskin, 61, 76
  silk, 25, 32, 47, 64, 70, 76, 93, 100, 102, 110. *see also* Maharani silk
  silk chiffon, 64, 77
  suede, polyester, 29, 71, 98
  Tencel®, 64, 97, 98
  Trentine, 25
fashion shows, 78, 81
Feldman, Barbara (Opperman), 19
Feldman, Janice (Moody Robinson)
  company, 11, 19, 29, 57
  designer, 26, 60, 61, 70, 88
Feldman, Jerry, 51, 59, 90
Feldman, Josh
  background, 32, 33, 52
  company, 22, 61, 64, 96, 98, 112
  engineered prints, 63, 64, 100
  on his father, 14, 19, 40, 51, 61, 64, 90
  manager, 12, 44, 46, 55, 82, 83, 94, 108–110
  print, 93
Feldman, June (Tatibouet), 31, 32, 51, 61, 62, 63
Feldman, Lisa, 82
Feldman, Mortimer, 27
  art, 17, 18, 40, 47
  Asian influence, 68–69
  color, 47, 51
  good taste, 18, 26, 29, 39
  high fashion, 78, 80
  Japanese influence, 29, 39–40, 68
  legacy, 12, 18
  manager, 26, 29, 31, 32, 46, 57, 103
  negotiator, 18, 34, 36, 40, 70
  prints, 44, 63, 64
  quality, 11, 54
Feldman, Richard, 20
fire sale, 31
Fisher, Jim, 96, 102

Foster, Bill, 27
Foster, Mary, 27
Frank, Alison, 12
French seams, 56, 97
Fujii, Juline, 94, 97
furoshiki, 68, 72, 80

G
Garys, 96
Glamour, 23
Goodman, Jesse, 98
greige goods, 34

H
Harley-Davidson resort apparel, 87
Harper's Bazaar, 23
Hawaiian Fashion Guild, 27, 28, 32, 81
Hawaiian garment manufacturers
    Hilo Hattie, 12, 40, 103
    Iolani, 26
    Kahala, 26, 27, 29
    Kamehameha, 26
    Malia, 26, 27
    Shaheen, Alfred, 13, 26
    Sun Fashions, 28
Hilo Hattie, 12, 40, 103
HongKong Standard, 80
Honolulu Advertiser, 28
Honolulu Star-Bulletin, 12, 31, 72
Hope, Dale, 103
Hope, Howard, 28

I
I. Magnin, 11, 23, 61, 73
Ice Capades, 77
InStyle, 90
interlining, 56
International Market Place, 68
Iolani, 26
Island Business, 12

J
jacquard, 47, 97, 98, 110
Japan, 39–40
Japanese influence, 29, 39–40, 68–69. *see also* Asian influence
jersey, 64, 98

K
Kahala, 26, 27, 29
Kamehameha, 26
Kapuakela, Doreen, 65
Karpowicz, Agatha, 56
Kawamoto, Fran, 53
Kea, Baba, 78
keeps, 42
Kojoma, A., 36
Kotomori, Amos, 32, 80, 81

L
Lapidus, Ted, 80
Lauren, Ralph, 79
Liberty House, 18, 29, 32, 62, 97
licensed products, 87
Life, 23
Lindquist, Mark, 102, 103
Lord & Taylor, 11, 23, 26
loungewear line, 31, 61, 62–63

M
MacRae, Don, 52, 55
MacRae, Karen, 20
Macy's, 18
Mademoiselle, 23, 62
Maharani silk, 61. *see also* silk
Malia, 26, 27
Marshall Field, 11, 81
matched fronts, 54, 55, 98
matched pockets, 54, 98
men's shirt. *see* shirts
men's wear line, 29, 32, 94–103
mirrored prints, 55
Moberg, Haruko, 29, 30, 71
Morketter, Stan, 32

N
National Cotton Council, 62
National Federation of Independent Business, 112
Neiman Marcus, 11, 23, 73, 81
Nichimen, 34, 36
Nik-Nik, 64, 100
Nordstrom, 11, 81, 94, 96
Norfleet, Nat, Jr., 29
Norfleet, Nat, Sr., 27

O
Odenberg, Ralph, 108, 111
OK!, 90
Otake, Eileen, 83

P
Pacific Business News, 98
Phillips-Van Heusen, 43
Pier 7 factory (Honolulu Harbor), 20
piqué, 25
placement prints, 55
Poliandro, Leonard, 26, 39, 40
Polo, 79
polyester suede. *see* suede, polyester
Polyplush, 61, 80
Primo Brewery factory (Cooke St.), 20, 29, 30

print process, 42–44
prints. *see also* engineered prints
    Arabesque, 42, 61, 64, 77, 82
    Cho-Cho, 70
    Crescendo, 61
    Daisy-Mae, 61
    Fossil, 93
    Furoshiki, 70
    Gaiety, 61
    Hampton, 61
    Happiness, 61
    Horizon, 61
    Imperial Screen, 76
    Kabuki, 42, 70
    Kenya, 42
    Lido, 61
    Lotus, 70
    Mandarin, 93
    Marquesas, 42, 102
    Mediterranean, 93
    Midnight, 93
    Montego, 61
    Murano, 42, 93, 102
    Orient Express, 93
    Orientale, 70
    Origami, 70
    Pacifica, 61
    Patio, 42, 49, 100
    Picasso, 61
    Plaza, 42
    Pop!, 42
    Rio, 42, 61
    Roma, 61
    Seafrost, 42
    Shibui, 42, 70
    Skoshi, 11
    Sunrise, 42
    Tegaki, 42, 70–72
    Trumpetini, 93
    Zabuton, 70
prints (types)
    mirrored prints, 55
    placement prints, 55

Q
quality control, 51, 57
Quonset hut factory (Beretania St.), 20

R
rayon, 56, 72, 100, 102
Renshaw, Amy, 42, 44, 47
repeat, 44, 55, 64
Romig, Jim, 12, 40, 103

S
Sakowitz, 73, 81
Saks Fifth Avenue, 11, 26, 27, 61, 81, 90, 100
Scoggins, Kim, 34, 36, 46, 53, 71
Shaheen, Alfred, 13, 26
sharkskin, 61, 76
Shere Khan, 32
shirts, 29, 54, 55, 63, 64, 72, 96, 97, 98
Shogun, 72
showrooms, 30, 62, 94, 109
silk, 25, 32, 47, 64, 70, 76, 93, 100, 102. *see also* Maharani silk
silk chiffon, 64, 77
Smoyer, Doug, 64
Snyder, Diane, 68
styles
    cocktail shorty, 61
    Galaxy, 78
    Paravent, 78
    Razzmatazz, 78
    toga mu'u, 61
    Tori Taper, 61
suede, polyester, 29, 71, 98
Sun Fashions, 28
Sunday Star-Bulletin and Advertiser, 78
swimsuits, 86–89

T
Taum, Bobby, 22
Tegaki line, 70–72
Tencel®, 64, 97, 98
textiles. *see* fabrics
Tori tops, 68–69
Town & Country, 23
Tree, Penelope, 23
Trentine, 25
Troedson, Mark, 32, 100, 102

V
Vancouver Sun, 58

W
Wickland, Tori, 20, 88
Women's Wear Daily, 90
women's wear line, 60–64, 76–77, 81

Y
Yamada, Ellie, 52, 54, 55, 56, 57
Yamamoto, Kansai, 80
Yep, Lauren, 18, 29, 98